The

Periodic

Table

50 YEARS OF PUBLISHING
1945-1995

The

Periodic

Table

Primo Levi

Translated from the Italian by
Raymond Rosenthal

SCHOCKEN BOOKS   NEW YORK

Library of Congress Cataloging-in-Publication Data
Levi, Primo
        The periodic table
        Translation of: Il sistema periodico.
        I. Title.
PQ4872.E8S513 1984   854'.914   84-5453
ISBN 0-8052-1041-5

Manufactured in the United States of America
['95] 9   8   7

CONTENTS

Ibergekumene tsores iz gut tsu dertseylin.
Troubles overcome are good to tell.
—Yiddish Proverb

The

Periodic

Table

ARGON

There are the so-called inert gases in the air we breathe. They bear curious Greek names of erudite derivation which mean "the New," "the Hidden," "the Inactive," and "the Alien." They are indeed so inert, so satisfied with their condition, that they do not interfere in any chemical reaction, do not combine with any other element, and for precisely this reason have gone undetected for centuries. As late as 1962 a diligent chemist after long and ingenious efforts succeeded in forcing the Alien (xenon) to combine fleetingly with extremely avid and lively fluorine, and the feat seemed so extraordinary that he was given a Nobel prize. They are also called the noble gases—and here there's room for discussion as to whether all noble gases are really inert and all inert gases are noble. And, finally, they are also called rare gases, even though one of them, argon (the Inactive), is present in the air in the considerable proportion of 1 percent, that is, twenty or thirty times more abundant than carbon dioxide, without which there would not be a trace of life on this planet.

The little that I know about my ancestors presents many similarities to these gases. Not all of them were materially inert, for that was not granted them. On the contrary, they were—or had to be—quite active, in order to earn a living and because of a reigning morality that held that "he who does not work shall not eat." But there is no doubt that they were inert in their inner spirits, inclined to disinterested speculation, witty discourses, elegant, sophisticated, and gratuitous discussion. It can hardly be by chance that all the deeds attributed to them, though quite various, have in common a touch of the static, an attitude of dignified abstention, of voluntary (or accepted) relegation to the margins of the great river of life. Noble, inert, and rare: their history is quite poor when compared to that of other illustrious Jewish communities in Italy and Europe. It appears that they arrived in Piedmont about 1500, from Spain by way of Provence, as seems proven by certain typical toponymic surnames, such as Bedarida-Bédarrides, Momigliano-Montmélian, Segre (this is a tributary of the Ebro which flows past Lérida in northeastern Spain), Foà-Foix, Cavaglion-Cavaillon, Migliau-Millau; the name of the town Lunel near the mouth of the Rhône between Montpellier and Nîmes was translated into the Hebrew *yareakh* ("moon"; *luna* in Italian), and from this derived the Jewish-Piedmontese surname Jarach.

Rejected or given a less than warm welcome in Turin, they settled in various agricultural localities in southern Piedmont, introducing there the technology of making silk, though without ever getting beyond, even in their most flourishing periods, the status of an extremely tiny minority. They were never much loved or much hated; stories of unusual persecutions have not been handed down. Nevertheless, a wall of suspicion, of undefined hostility and mockery, must have kept them substantially separated from the rest of the population, even several decades after the emancipation of 1848 and the consequent flow into the cities, if what my father told me of his childhood in Bene Vagienna is true. His contemporaries, he said, on coming out of school used to mock him without malice, greeting him with the corner of their jackets gathered in their fists to resemble a donkey's ear and chanting, "Pig's ear, donkey's ear, give 'em to the Jew that's here." The allusion to the ear is arbitrary, and the gesture was originally the sacrilegious parody of the greeting that pious Jews would exchange in synagogue when called up to read the Torah, showing each other the hem of the prayer shawl whose tassels, minutely prescribed by ritual as to number, length, and form, are replete with mystical and religious significance. But by now those kids were unaware of the origin of their gesture. I remember here, in passing, that the vilification of the prayer shawl is as old as anti-Semitism—from those shawls, taken from deportees, the SS would make underwear which then was distributed to the Jews imprisoned in the *Lager*.

As is always the case, the rejection was mutual. The minority erected a symmetrical barrier against all of Christianity (*goyim*, *narelim*, "Gentiles," the "uncircumcised"), reproducing on a provincial scale and against a pacifically bucolic background the epic and Biblical situation of the chosen people. This fundamental dislocation fed the good-natured wit of our uncles (*barbe* in the dialect of Piedmont) and our aunts (*magne*, also in the dialect): wise, tobacco-smelling patriarchs and domestic household queens, who would still proudly describe themselves as "the people of Israel."

As for this term "uncle," it is appropriate here to warn the reader immediately that it must be understood in a very broad sense. It is the custom among us to call any old relation uncle, even if he is a distant relation, and since all or almost all of the old persons in the community are in the long run relations, the result is that the number of uncles is very large. And then in the case of the uncles and aunts who reach an extremely old age (a frequent event: we are a long-lived people, since the time of

Noah), the attribute *barba* ("uncle"), or, respectively, *magna* ("aunt") tends gradually to merge with the name, and, with the concurrence of ingenious diminutives and an unsuspected phonetic analogy between Hebrew and the Piedmontese dialect, become fixed in complex, strange-sounding appellations, which are handed down unchanged from generation to generation along with the events, memories, and sayings of those who had borne them for many long years. Thus came into existence Barbaiòtô (Uncle Elijah), Barbasachín (Uncle Isaac), Magnaiéta (Aunt Maria), Barbamôisín (Uncle Moses, about whom it is said that he had the quack pull his two lower incisors so as to hold the stem of his pipe more comfortably), Barbasmelín (Uncle Samuel), Magnavigaia (Aunt Abigail, who as a bride had entered Saluzzo mounted on a white mule, coming up the ice-covered Po River from Carmagnola), Magnafôriña (Aunt Zepora, from the Hebrew *Tsippora* which means "bird": a splendid name). Uncle Jacob must have belonged to an even remoter period. He had been to England to purchase cloth and so "wore a checked suit"; his brother Barbapartín (Uncle Bonaparte, a name still common among the Jews, in memory of the first ephemeral emancipation bestowed by Napoleon), had fallen from his rank as uncle because the Lord, blessed be He, had given him so unbearable a wife that he had had himself baptized, became a monk, and left to work as a missionary in China, so as to be as far away from her as possible.

Grandmother Bimba was very beautiful, wore a boa of ostrich feathers, and was a baroness. She and her entire family had been made barons by Napoleon, because they had lent him money (*manòd*).

Barbabarônín (Uncle Aaron) was tall, robust, and had radical ideas; he had run away from Fossano to Turin and had worked at many trades. He had been signed up by the Carignano Theater as an extra in *Don Carlos* and had written to his family to come for the opening. Uncle Nathan and Aunt Allegra came and sat in the gallery; when the curtain went up and Aunt Allegra saw her son armed like a Philistine, she shouted at the top of her lungs: "Aaron, what are you doing! Put that sword down!"

Barbamiclín was simple; in Acqui he was respected and protected because the simple are the children of God and no one should call them fools. But they called him "turkey planter" since the time a *rashan* (an unbeliever) had made a fool of him by leading him to believe that turkeys (*bibini*) are sowed like peach trees, by planting the feathers in furrows, and that then they grow on the branches. In any event, the turkey had a curiously important place in this witty, mild, and orderly family world, perhaps because, being presumptuous, clumsy, and wrathful, it expresses the opposite qualities and lends itself to being an object of ridicule; or perhaps, more simply, because at its expense a famous, semi-ritual turkey meatball was confected at Passover. For example, Uncle Pacifico also raised a turkey-hen and had become very attached to her. Across the way from him lived Signor Lattes, who was a musician. The turkey clucked and disturbed Signor Lattes; he begged Uncle Pacifico to silence his turkey. My uncle replied, "Your orders will be carried out; Signora Turkey keep quiet."

Uncle Gabriele was a rabbi and therefore he was known as Barba Moréno, that is, "Uncle Our Teacher." Old and nearly blind, he would return on foot, under the blazing sun, from Verzuolo to Saluzzo. He saw a cart come by, stopped it, and asked for a ride; but then, while talking to the driver, it gradually dawned on him that this was a hearse, which was carrying a dead Christian to the cemetery: an abominable thing, since, as it is written in Ezekiel 44:25, a priest who touches a dead man, or even simply enters the room in which a dead person is lying, is contaminated and impure for seven days. He leaped to his feet and cried: "I'm traveling with a *pegartà*, with a dead woman! Driver, stop the cart!"

Gnôr Grassiadiô and Gnôr Côlômbô were two friendly enemies who, according to the legend, had lived from time immemorial face to face on the two sides of an alleyway in the town of Moncalvo. Gnôr Grassiadiô was a Mason and very rich. He was a bit ashamed of being a Jew and had married a *goyà*, that is, a Christian, with blond hair so long it touched the ground, who cuckolded him. This *goyà*, although really a *goyà*, was called Magna Ausilia, which indicates a certain degree of acceptance on the part of the epigones; she was the daughter of a sea captain who had presented Gnôr Grassiadiô with a large, varicolored parrot which came from Guyana and would say in Latin, "Know thyself." Gnôr Côlômbô was poor and a Mazzinian. When the parrot arrived he bought a crow without a feather on its back and taught it to speak. When the parrot croaked, "*Nosce te ipsum*," the crow answered, "Wise up."

But as for Uncle Gabriele's *pegartà*, Gnôr Grassiadiô's *goyà*, Nona Bimba's *manòd*, and the *havertà* of which we will speak, an explanation is required. *Havertà* is a Hebrew word, crippled in both its form and meaning and quite suggestive. Actually it is an arbitrary feminine form of *haver*, which equals "companion" and means "maid," but it contains the accessory notion of a woman of low extraction and of different customs and beliefs that one is forced to harbor under one's roof; by inclination a *havertà* is not very clean and is ill-mannered, and by definition she is malevolently curious about the customs and conversations of the masters of the house, so much so as to force them to use a particular jargon in her presence, to which, besides all the others mentioned above, the term *havertà* itself obviously belongs. This jargon has now almost disappeared; a few generations back it still numbered a few hundred words and locutions, consisting for the most part of Hebrew roots with Piedmontese endings and inflections. Even a hasty examination points to its dissimulative and underground function, a crafty language meant to be employed when speaking about *goyim* in the presence of *goyim*; or also, to reply boldly with insults and curses that are not to be understood, against the regime of restriction and oppression which they (the *goyim*) had established.

Its historical interest is meager, since it was never spoken by more than a few thousand people; but its human interest is great, as are all languages on the frontier and in transition. In fact it contains an admirable comic force, which springs from the contrast between the texture of the discourse, which is the rugged, sober, and laconic Piedmontese dialect, never written except on a bet, and the Hebrew inlay, snatched from the language of the fathers, sacred and solemn, geologic, polished smooth by the millennia like the bed of a glacier. But this contrast reflects another, the essential conflict of the Judaism of the Diaspora, scattered among the Gentiles, that is, the *goyim*, torn between their divine vocation and the daily misery of existence; and still another, even more general, which is inherent in the human condition, since man is a centaur, a tangle of flesh and mind, divine inspiration and dust. The Jewish people, after the dispersion, have lived this conflict for a long time and dolorously, and have drawn from it, side by side with its wisdom, also its laughter, which in fact is missing in the Bible and the Prophets. It pervades Yiddish, and, within its modest limits, it also pervades the bizarre speech of our fathers of this earth,* which I want to set down here before it disappears: a skeptical, good-natured speech, which only to a careless examination could appear blasphemous, whereas it is rich with an affectionate and dignified intimacy with God—Nôssgnôr ("Our Lord"), Adonai Eloenó ("Praise be the Lord"), Cadòss Barôkhu ("Dear Lord").

Its humiliated roots are evident. For example, there are missing, because useless, words for "sun," "man," and "city," while words are present for "night," "to hide," "money," "prison," "dream" (the last, though, used almost exclusively in the locution *bahalom*, "in a dream," to be added jokingly to an affirmation, and to be understood by one's interlocutor, and by him alone, as its contrary), "to steal," "to hang," and suchlike. Besides this, there exist a good number of disparaging words, used sometimes to judge persons but more typically employed, for example, between wife and husband in front of a Christian

*This is an allusion to the Christian prayer that begins, "Our Father, who art in heaven."

shopkeeper's counter when uncertain about the purchase. We mention: *n saròd*, the royal plural, no longer understood as such, of the Hebrew *tsara*, which means "misfortune" and is used to describe a piece of goods or a person of scant value; there also exists its graceful diminutive, *saròdïnn*, and at the same time I would not want forgotten the ferocious linkage *saròd e senssa manód,* used by the marriage broker (*marosav*) to describe ugly girls without dowries; *hasirud*, an abstract collective from *hasir*, which means "pig" and therefore is more or less equivalent to "filth, piggishness." It should be noted that the sound "u" (French) does not exist in Hebrew; instead there is the ending "ut" (with the Italian "u"), which serves to coin abstract terms (for example, *malkhut*, "kingdom"), but it lacks the strongly disparaging connotation it had in jargon usage. Another use, typical and obvious, of these and similar terms was in the store, between the owner and the clerks and against the customers. In the Piedmont of the last century the trade in cloth was often in Jewish hands, and from it was born a kind of specialized sub-jargon which, transmitted by the clerks become owners in their turn, and not necessarily Jews, has spread to many stores in the field and still lives, spoken by people who are quite surprised if by chance they happen to find out that they are using Hebrew words. Some, for example, still use the expression *na vesta a kinim* to describe a polka-dot dress: now, *kinim* are lice, the third of the ten scourges of Egypt, enumerated and chanted in the ritual of the Jewish Passover.

There is also a rather large assortment of not very decent terms, to be used not only with their real meaning in front of children but also instead of curses, in which case, compared to the corresponding Italian and Piedmontese terms, they offer, besides the already mentioned advantage of not being understood, also that of relieving the heart without abrading the mouth.

Certainly more interesting for the student of customs are the few terms that allude to things pertaining to the Catholic faith. In this case, the originally Hebraic form is corrupted much more profoundly, and this for two reasons: in the first place, secrecy was rigorously necessary here because their comprehension by Gentiles could have entailed the danger of being charged with sacrilege; in the second place, the distortion in this case acquires the precise aim of denying, obliterating the sacral content of the word, and thus divesting it of all supernatural virtue. For the same reason, in all languages the Devil is named with many appellations of an allusive and euphemistic character, which make it possible to refer to him without proferring his name. The church (Catholic) was called *tônevà*, a word whose origins I have not been able to reconstruct, and which probably takes from Hebrew only its sound; while the synagogue, with proud modesty, was simply called the *scola* ("school"), the place where one learns and is brought up. In a parallel instance, the rabbi is not described with the word *rabbi* or *rabbenu* ("our rabbi") but as *morénô* ("our teacher"), or *khakhàm* ("the wise man"). In fact in "school" one is not afflicted by the hateful *khaltrúm* of the Gentiles: *khaltrúm*, or *khantrúm*, is the ritual and bigotry of the Catholics, intolerable because polytheistic and above all because swarming with images ("Thou shalt have no other gods before me; Thou shalt not make unto thee any graven image . . . and shalt not bow down thyself to them," Exodus 20:3) and therefore idolatrous. For this term too, steeped in execration, the origin is obscure, almost certainly not Hebraic; but in other Jewish-Italian jargons there is the adjective *khalto*, in the sense precisely of "bigot" and used chiefly to describe the Christian worshiper of images.

A-issá is the Madonna (simply, that is, "the woman"). Completely cryptic and indecipherable—and that was to be foreseen—is the term *Odo*, with which, when it was absolutely unavoidable, one alluded to Christ, lowering one's voice and looking around with circumspection; it is best to speak of Christ as little as possible because the myth of the God-killing people dies hard.

Many other terms were drawn exactly as is from the ritual and the holy books, which Jews born in the last century read more or less fluently in the original Hebrew, and more often than not understood, at least partially; but, in jargon usage, they tended to deform or arbitrarily enlarge the semantic area. From the root *shafòkh*, which is equivalent to "pour" and appears in Psalm 79 ("Pour out Thy wrath upon the heathen that have not recognized Thee, and upon the kingdoms that have not invoked Thy name"), our ancient mothers have taken the homely expression *fé sefòkh*, that is, "to make *sefòkh*," with which one described with delicacy the vomit of infants. From *rúakh*, plural *rukhòd*, which means "breath," illustrious term that can be read in the dark and admirable second verse of Genesis ("The wind of the Lord breathed upon the face of the waters") was taken *tiré 'n rúakh*, "make a wind," in its diverse physiological significances, where one catches a glimpse of the Biblical intimacy of the Chosen People with its Creator. As an example of practical application, there has been handed down the saying of Aunt Regina, seated with Uncle David in the Café Florio on Via Po: *"Davidin, bat la cana, c'as sento nen le rukhòd!"* ("David, thump your cane, so they don't hear your winds!"), which attests to a conjugal relationship of affectionate intimacy. As for the cane, it was at that time a symbol of social status, just as traveling first class on the railroad can be today. My father, for example, owned two canes, a bamboo cane for weekdays, and another of malacca with a silver-plated handle for Sunday. He did not use the cane to lean on (he had no need for that), but rather to twirl jovially in the air and to shoo insolent dogs from his path: in short, as a scepter to distinguish him from the vulgar crowd.

Barakhà is the benediction a pious Jew is expected to pronounce more than a hundred times a day, and he does so with profound joy, since by doing so he carries on a thousand-year-old dialogue with the Eternal, who in every *barakhà* is praised and thanked for His gifts. Grandfather Leonin was my great-grandfather. He lived at Casale Monferrato and had flat feet; the alley in front of his house was paved with cobblestones, and he suffered when he walked on it. One morning he came out of his house and found the alley paved with flagstones, and he exclaimed from the depths of his heart, " 'N abrakha a coi goyim c'a l'an fait i losi!" ("A blessing on those unbelievers who made these paving stones!"). As a curse, however, there was the curious linkage medà meshônà, which literally means "strange death" but actually is an imitation of the Piedmontese assident, that is, in plain Italian, "may he drop dead." To the same Grandpa Leonin is attributed the inexplicable imprecation "C'ai takeissa 'na medà meshônà faita a paraqua" ("May he have an accident shaped like an umbrella").

Nor could I forget Barbaricô, close in space and time, so much so that he just missed (only by a single generation) being my uncle in the strict sense of the word. Of him I preserve a personal and thus articulated and complex memory. Not figé dans une attitude, like that of the mythical characters I have mentioned up until now. The comparison to inert gases with which these pages start fits Barbaricô like a glove.

He had studied medicine and had become a good doctor, but he did not like the world. That is, he liked men, and especially women, the meadows, the sky; but not hard work, the racket made by wagons, the intrigues for the sake of a career, the hustling for one's daily bread, commitments, schedules, and due dates; nothing in short of all that characterized the feverish life of the town of Casale Monferrato in 1890. He would have liked to escape, but he was too lazy to do so. His friends and a woman who loved him, and whom he tolerated with distracted benevolence, persuaded him to take the test for the position of ship's doctor aboard a transatlantic steamer. He won the competition easily, made a single voyage from Genoa to New York, and on his return to Genoa handed in his resignation because in America "there was too much noise."

After that he settled in Turin. He had several women, all of whom wanted to redeem and marry him, but he regarded both matrimony and an equipped office and the regular exercise of his profession as too much of a commitment. Around about

1930 he was a timid little old man, shriveled and neglected, frightfully nearsighted; he lived with a big, vulgar *goyà*, from whom he tried at intervals and feebly to free himself, and whom he described from time to time as *'na sôtià* ("a nut"), *'na hamortà* ("a donkey"), and *'na gran beemà* ("a great beast"), but without acrimony and indeed with a vein of inexplicable tenderness. This *goyà* even wanted to have him *samdà* *"baptized"* *(literally, "destroyed")*: a thing he had always refused to do, not out of religious conviction but out of indifference and a lack of initiative.

Barbaricô had no less than twelve brothers and sisters, who described his companion with the ironic and cruel name of Magna Morfina (Aunt Morphine): ironic because the woman, poor thing, being a *goyà* and childless could not be a *magna* except in an extremely limited sense, and indeed the term *magna* was to be understood as its exact opposite, a non-*magna*, someone excluded and cut off from the family; and cruel because it contained a probably false and at any rate pitiless allusion to a certain exploitation on her part of Barbaricô's prescription blanks.

The two of them lived in a filthy and chaotic attic room on Borgo Vanchiglia. My uncle was a fine doctor, full of human wisdom and diagnostic intuition, but he spent the entire day stretched out on his cot reading books and old newspapers: he was an attentive reader, eclectic and untiring, with a long memory, although myopia forced him to hold the print three inches from his eyeglasses, which were as thick as the bottom of a beer glass. He only got up when a patient sent for him, which often happened because he almost never asked to be paid; his patients were the poor people on the outskirts of town, from whom he would accept as recompense a half-dozen eggs, or some lettuce from the garden, or even a pair of worn-out shoes. He visited his patients on foot because he did not have the money for the streetcar; when on the street he caught a dim view, through the mist of his myopia, of a girl, he went straight up to her and to her surprise examined her carefully, circling from a foot away. He ate almost nothing, and in a general way he had no needs; he died at over ninety, with discretion and dignity.

Like Barbaricô in her rejection of the world was Grandmother Fina, one of the four sisters whom everyone called Fina: this first name singularity was owed to the fact that the four girls had been sent successively to the same wet nurse in Bra whose name was Delfina and who called all her "nurslings" by that name. Grandmother Fina lived at Carmagnola, in an apartment on the second floor, and did splendid crochet work. At eighty-six she had a slight indisposition, a *caodana*, as ladies used to have in those days and today mysteriously no longer do: from then on, for twenty years—that is, until her death—she never left her room; on the Sabbath, from her little terrace overflowing with geraniums, fragile and pale, she waved her hand to the people who came out of the *scola* ("synagogue"). But she must have been quite different in her youth, if what is told about her is true: namely, that her husband having brought to the house as a guest the Rabbi of Moncalvo, an erudite and illustrious man, she had served him, without his knowing, a pork cutlet, since there was nothing else in the pantry. Her brother Barbaraflín (Raphael), who before his promotion to Barba was known as *l fieul d' Moise 'd Celin* ("the son of the Moses of Celin"), now at a mature age and very rich because of the money earned from army supplies had fallen in love with the very beautiful Dolce Valabrega from Gassino; he did not dare declare himself, wrote her love letters that he never mailed, and then wrote impassioned replies to himself.

Marchín, too, an ex-uncle, had an unhappy love. He became enamored of Susanna (which means "lily" in Hebrew), a brisk, pious woman, the depository of a century-old recipe for the confection of goose sausage; these sausages are made by using the neck of the bird itself as a casing, and as a result in the Lassòn Acodesh (the "holy tongue," that is, in the jargon we are discussing), more than three synonyms for "neck" have survived. The first, *mahané*, is neuter and has a technical, 15 generic use; the second, *savàr*, is used only in metaphors, as "at breakneck speed"; and the third, *khanèc*, extremely allusive and suggestive, refers to the neck as a vital passage, which can be obstructed, occluded, or severed; and it is used in imprecations, such as "may it stick in your neck"; *khanichésse* means "to hang oneself." In any event, Marchín was Susanna's clerk and assistant; both in the mysterious kitchen-workshop and in the store, on whose shelves were promiscuously placed sausages, holy furnishings, amulets, and prayer books. Susanna turned him down and Marchín got his abominable revenge by selling the recipe for the sausage to a *goy*. One must think that this *goy* did not appreciate its value, since after Susanna's death (which took place in a legendary past) it has no longer been possible to find in commerce goose sausage worthy of the name and tradition. Because of this contemptible retaliation, Uncle Marchín lost his right to be called an uncle.

Remotest of all, portentously inert, wrapped in a thick shroud of legend and the incredible, fossilized in his quality as an uncle, was Barbabramín of Chieri, the uncle of my maternal grandmother. When still young he was already rich, having bought from the aristocrats of the place numerous farms between Chieri and the Asti region; relying on the inheritance they would receive from him, his relations squandered their wealth on banquets, balls, and trips to Paris. Now it happened that his mother, Aunt Milca (the Queen) fell sick, and after much argument with her husband was led to agree to hire a *havertà*, that is, a maid, which she had flatly refused to do until then: in fact, quite prescient, she did not want women around the house. Punctually, Barbabramín was overcome with love for this *havertà*, probably the first female less than saintly whom he had an opportunity to get close to.

Her name has not been handed down, but instead a few attributes. She was opulent and beautiful and possesed splendid *khlaviòd* ("breasts"): the term is unknown in classic Hebrew, where, however, *khalàv* means "milk.") She was of course a *goyà*, was insolent, and did not know how to read or write; but she was an excellent cook. She was a peasant, 'na ponaltà, and went barefoot in the house. But this is exactly what my uncle fell in love with: her ankles, her straightforward speech, and the dishes she cooked. He did not say anything to the girl but told his father and mother that he intended to marry her; his parents went wild with rage and my uncle took to his bed. He stayed there for twenty-two years.

As to what Uncle Bramín did during those years, there are divergent accounts. There is no doubt that for a good part he slept and gambled them away; it is known for certain that he went to pot economically because "he did not clip the coupons" of the treasury bonds, and because he had entrusted the administration of the farms to a *mamser* ("bastard"), who had sold them for a song to a front man of his; in line with Aunt Milca's premonition, my uncle thus dragged the whole family into ruin, and to this day they bewail the consequences.

It is also said that he read and studied and that, considered at last knowledgeable and just, received at his bedside delegations of Chieri notables and settled disputes; it is also said that the path to that same bed was not unknown to that same *havertà*, and that at least during the first years my uncle's voluntary seclusion was interrupted by nocturnal sorties to go and play billiards in the café below. But at any rate he stayed in bed for almost a quarter of a century, and when Aunt Milca and Uncle Solomon died he married a *goyà* and took her into his bed definitively, because he was by now so weak that his legs no longer held him up. He died poor but rich in years and fame and in the peace of the spirit in 1883.

Susanna of the goose sausage was the cousin of Grandmother Malia, my paternal grandmother, who survives in the figure of an overdressed, tiny vamp in some studio poses executed around 1870, and as a wrinkled, short-tempered, slovenly, and fabulously deaf old lady in my most distant childhood memories. Still today, inexplicably, the highest shelves of the closets give us back her precious relics, shawls of black lace embroidered with iridescent spangles, noble silk embroideries, a marten fur muff mangled by four generations of moths, massive silver tableware engraved with her initials: as though, after almost fifty years, her restless spirit still visited our house.

In her youth she was known as "the heartbreaker"; she was left a widow very early and the rumor spread that my grandfather had killed himself in desperation over her infidelities. She raised alone three boys in a Spartan manner and made them study; but at an advanced age she gave in and married an old Christian doctor, a majestic, taciturn, bearded man, and from then on inclined to stinginess and oddity, although in youth she had been regally prodigal, as beautiful, much loved women usually are. With the passing of the years she cut herself off completely from any family affections (which in any case she must never have felt very deeply). She lived with the doctor on Via Po, in a gloomy, dark apartment, barely warmed in winter by just a small Franklin stove, and she no longer threw out anything, because everything might eventually come in handy: not even the cheese rinds or the foil on chocolates, with which she made silver balls to be sent to missions to "free a little black boy." Perhaps out of a fear of making a mistake in her definitive choice, on alternate days she attended the *scola* on Via Pius the Fifth and the parish church of Sant' Ottavio, and it appears that she would even go sacrilegiously to confession. She died past eighty in 1928, watched over by a chorus of unkempt neighbors, all dressed in black and, like her, half demented, led by a witch whose name was Madame Scilimberg. Even though tormented by her renal occlusion, my grandmother kept a sharp eye on Scilimberg until her last breath for fear she might find the *maftekh* ("key") hidden under the mattress and carry off the *manòd* ("money") and the *hafassim* ("jewels"), all of which turned out to be fake.

At her death, her sons and daughters-in-law spent weeks, filled with dismay and disgust, picking through the mountains of household debris with which the apartment overflowed. Grandmother Malia had indiscriminately saved exquisite objects and revolting garbage. From severe carved walnut closets issued armies of bedbugs dazzled by the light, and then linen sheets never used, and other sheets patched and threadbare, worn so thin as to be transparent, curtains, and reversible damask bedspreads; a collection of stuffed hummingbirds which as soon as touched fell into dust; in the cellar lay hundreds of bottles of precious wines which had turned into vinegar. They found eight overcoats belonging to the doctor, brand new, stuffed with mothballs, and the only one she had allowed him to use, all patches and darnings, its collar slick with grease and a Masonic emblem hidden in its pocket.

I remember almost nothing about her, whom my father called Maman (also in the third person) and loved to describe, with his eager taste for the bizarre, slightly tempered by a veil of filial piety. Every Sunday morning my father took me on foot in a visit to Grandmother Malia: we walked slowly down Via Po, and he stopped to caress all the cats, sniff at all the truffles, and leaf through all the secondhand books. My father was *l'ingegné* ("the engineer"), with his pockets always bulging with books and known to all the pork butchers because he checked with his logarithmic ruler the multiplication for the prosciutto purchase. Not that he purchased this last item with a carefree heart: superstitious rather than religious, he felt ill at ease at breaking the *kasherut* rules, but he liked prosciutto so much that, faced by the temptation of a shop window, he yielded every time, sighing, cursing under his breath, and watching me out of the corner of his eye, as if he feared my judgment or hoped for my complicity.

When we arrived at the tenebrous landing of the apartment on Via Po, my father rang the bell, and when my grandmother came to open the door he would shout in her ear: "He's at the head of his class!" My grandmother would let us in with visible reluctance and guide us through a string of dusty, uninhabited rooms, one of which, studded with sinister instruments, was the doctor's semi-abandoned office. One hardly ever saw the doctor, nor did I certainly want to see him, ever since the day on which I had surprised my father telling my mother that, when they brought him stammering children to be treated, he would cut the fillet of skin under the tongue with his scissors. When we got to the good living room, my grandmother would dig out of some recess the box of chocolates, always the same box, and offer me one. The chocolate was worm-eaten, and with great embarrassment I would quickly hide it away in my pocket.

H Y D R O G E N

It was January. Enrico came to call for me right after dinner: his
brother had gone up into the mountains and had left him the
keys to the laboratory. I dressed in a flash and joined him on the
street.

During the walk I learned that his brother had not really left
him the keys: this was simply a compendious formulation, a
euphemism, the sort of thing you said to someone ready to
understand. His brother, contrary to his habit, had not hidden
the keys, nor had he taken them with him; what's more, he had
forgotten to repeat to Enrico the prohibition against appropriat-
ing these same keys, and the punishment threatened should
Enrico disobey. To put it bluntly, there were the keys, after

months of waiting; Enrico and I were determined not to pass up the opportunity.

We were sixteen, and I was fascinated with Enrico. He was not very active, and his scholastic output was pretty meager, but he had virtues that distinguished him from all the other members of the class, and he did things that nobody else did. He possessed a calm, stubborn courage, a precocious capacity to sense his own future and to give it weight and shape. He turned his back (but without contempt) on our interminable discussions, now Platonic, now Darwinian, later still Bergsonian; he was not vulgar, he did not boast of his virile attributes or his skill at sports, he never lied. He knew his limitations, but we never heard him say (as we all told each other, with the idea of currying comfort, or blowing off steam): "You know, I really think I'm an idiot."

He had a slow, foot-slogging imagination: he lived on dreams like all of us, but his dreams were sensible; they were obtuse, possible, contiguous to reality, not romantic, not cosmic. He did not experience my tormented oscillation between the heaven (of a scholastic or sports success, a new friendship, a rudimentary and fleeting love) and the hell (of a failing grade, a remorse, a brutal revelation of an inferiority which each time seemed eternal, definitive). His goals were always attainable. He dreamed of promotion and studied with patience things that did not interest him. He wanted a microscope and sold his racing bike to get it. He wanted to be a pole vaulter and went to the gym every evening for a year without making a fuss about it, breaking any bones, or tearing a ligament, until he reached the mark of 3.5 meters he had set himself, and then stopped. Later he wanted a certain woman and he got her; he wanted the money to live quietly and obtained it after ten years of boring, prosaic work.

We had no doubts: we would be chemists, but our expectations and hopes were quite different. Enrico asked chemistry, quite reasonably, for the tools to earn his living and have a secure life. I asked for something entirely different; for me

chemistry represented an indefinite cloud of future poten-
tialities which enveloped my life to come in black volutes torn
by fiery flashes, like those which had hidden Mount Sinai. Like
Moses, from that cloud I expected my law, the principle of
order in me, around me, and in the world. I was fed up with
books, which I still continued to gulp down with indiscreet
voracity, and searched for another key to the highest truths:
there must be a key, and I was certain that, owing to some
monstrous conspiracy to my detriment and the world's, I would
not get it in school. In school they loaded me with tons of
notions which I diligently digested, but which did not warm the
blood in my veins. I would watch the buds swell in spring, the
mica glint in the granite, my own hands, and I would say to
myself: "I will understand this, too, I will understand everything, but not the way *they* want me to. I will find a shortcut, I
will make a lock-pick, I will push open the doors."

It was enervating, nauseating, to listen to lectures on the
problem of being and knowing, when everything around us was
a mystery pressing to be revealed: the old wood of the benches,
the sun's sphere beyond the windowpanes and the roofs, the
vain flight of the pappus down in the June air. Would all the
philosophers and all the armies of the world be able to construct
this little fly? No, nor even understand it: this was a shame and
an abomination, another road must be found.

We would be chemists, Enrico and I. We would dredge the
bowels of the mystery with our strength, our talent: we would
grab Proteus by the throat, cut short his inconclusive
metamorphoses from Plato to Augustine, from Augustine to
Thomas, from Thomas to Hegel, from Hegel to Croce. We
would force him to speak.

This being our program, we could not afford to waste any
opportunities. Enrico's brother, a mysterious and choleric personage, about whom Enrico did not like to talk, was a chemistry
student, and he had installed a laboratory at the rear of a
courtyard, in a curious, narrow, twisting alleyway which
branched off Piazza della Crocetta and stood out in the obsessive

Turinese geometry like a rudimentary organ trapped in the evolved structure of a mammalian. The laboratory was also rudimentary: not in the sense of an atavistic vestige but in that of extreme poverty. There was a tiled workbench, very few glass receptacles, about twenty flasks with reagents, much dust and cobwebs, little light, and great cold. On our way we had discussed what we were going to do now that we had "gained access to the laboratory," but our ideas were confused.

It seemed to us an *embarras de richesses*, and it was instead a different embarrassment, deeper and more essential: an embarrassment tied to an ancient atrophy of ours, of our family, of our caste. What were we able to do with our hands? Nothing, or almost nothing. The women, yes—our mothers and grandmothers had lively, agile hands, they knew how to sew and cook, some even played the piano, painted with watercolors, embroidered, braided their hair. But we, and our fathers?

Our hands were at once coarse and weak, regressive, insensitive: the least trained part of our bodies. Having gone through the first fundamental experiences of play, they had learned to write, and that was all. They knew the convulsive grip around the branches of a tree, which we loved to climb out of a natural desire and also (Enrico and I) out of a groping homage and return to the origins of the species; but they were unfamiliar with the solemn, balanced weight of the hammer, the concentrated power of a blade, too cautiously forbidden us, the wise texture of wood, the similar and diverse pliability of iron, lead, and copper. If man is a maker, we were not men: we knew this and suffered from it.

The glass in the laboratory enchanted and intimidated us. Glass for us was that which one must not touch because it breaks, and yet, at a more intimate contact, revealed itself to be a substance different from all others, sui generis, full of mystery and caprice. It is similar in this to water, which also has no kindred forms: but water is bound to man, indeed to life, by a long-lasting familiarity, by a relationship of multifarious necessity, due to which its uniqueness is hidden beneath the crust of habit. Glass, however, is the work of man and has a more recent history. It was our first victim, or, better, our first adversary. In the Crocetta laboratory there was the usual lab glass, in various diameters and long and short sections, all covered with dust: we lit the Bunsen burner and set to work.

To bend the tube was easy. All you had to do was hold the section of tube steady over the flame: after a certain time the flame turned yellow and simultaneously the glass became weakly luminous. At this point the tube could be bent: the curve obtained was far from perfect, but in substance something took place, you could create a new, arbitrary shape; a potentiality became act. Wasn't this what Aristotle meant?

Now, a tube of copper or lead can also be bent, but we soon found out that the red-hot tube of glass possessed a unique virtue: when it had become pliable, you could, by quickly pulling on the two cold ends, pull it into very thin filaments, indeed unimaginably thin, so thin that it was drawn upwards by the current of hot air that rose from the flame. Thin and flexible, like silk. So then silk and cotton too, if obtainable in a massive form, could be as inflexible as glass? Enrico told me that in his grandfather's town the fishermen take silkworms, when they are already big and ready to form the pupa and, blind and clumsy, try to crawl up on the branches; they grab them, break them in two with their fingers, and pulling on the two stumps obtain a thread of silk, thick and coarse, which they then use as a fishing line. This fact, which I had no hesitation in believing, seemed to me both abominable and fascinating: abominable because of the cruel manner of that death, and the futile use of a natural portent; fascinating because of the straightforward and audacious act of ingenuity it presupposed on the part of its mythical inventor.

The glass tube could also be blown up; but this was much more difficult. You could close one end of a small tube: then blowing hard from the other end a bubble formed, very beauti-   *25* ful to look at and almost perfectly spherical but with absurdly thin walls. Even the slightest puff of breath in excess and the walls took on the iridescence of a soap bubble, and this was a certain sign of death: the bubble burst with a sharp little snap and its fragments were scattered over the floor with the tenuous rustle of eggshells. In some sense it was a just punishment; glass is glass, and it should not be expected to simulate the behavior of soapy water. If one forced the terms a bit, one could even see an Aesopian lesson in the event.

After an hour's struggle with the glass, we were tired and humiliated. We both had inflamed, dry eyes from looking too long at the red-hot glass, frozen feet, and fingers covered with burns. Besides, working with glass is not chemistry: we were in the laboratory with another goal. Our goal was to see with our eyes, to provoke with our hands, at least one of the phenomena which were described so offhandedly in our chemistry textbook. One could, for example, prepare nitrous oxide, which in Sestini and Funaro was still described with the not very proper and unserious term of laughing gas. Would it really be productive of laughter?

Nitrous oxide is prepared by cautiously heating ammonium nitrate. The latter did not exist in the lab; instead there was ammonia and nitric acid. We mixed them, unable to make any preliminary calculations until we had a neutral litmus reaction, as a result of which the mixture heated up greatly and emitted an abundance of white smoke; then we decided to bring it to a boil to eliminate the water. In a short time the lab was filled with a choking fog, which was not at all laughable; we broke off our attempt, luckily for us, because we did not know what can happen when this explosive salt is heated less than cautiously.

It was neither simple nor very amusing. I looked around and saw in a corner an ordinary dry battery. Here is something we could do: the electrolysis of water. It was an experiment with a guaranteed result, which I had already executed several times at home. Enrico would not be disappointed.

I put some water in a beaker, dissolved a pinch of salt in it, turned two empty jam jars upside down in the beaker; then found two rubber-coated copper wires, attached them to the battery's poles, and fitted the wire ends into the jam jars. A minuscule procession of air bubbles rose from the wire ends: indeed, observing them closely you could see that from the cathode about twice as much gas was being liberated as from the anode. I wrote the well-known equation on the blackboard, and explained to Enrico that what was written there was actually taking place. Enrico didn't seem too convinced, but by now it was dark and we were half frozen; we washed our hands, bought some slices of chestnut pudding and went home, leaving the electrolysis to continue on its own.

The next day we still had access. In pliant obsequiousness to theory, the cathode jar was almost full of gas; the anode jar was half full: I brought this to Enrico's attention, giving myself as much importance as I could, and trying to awaken the suspicion that, I won't say electrolysis, but its application as the confirmation of the law of definite proportions, was my invention, the fruit of patient experiments conducted secretly in my room. But Enrico was in a bad mood and doubted everything. "Who says that it's actually hydrogen and oxygen?" he said to me rudely. "And what if there's chlorine? Didn't you put in salt?"

The objection struck me as insulting: How did Enrico dare to doubt my statement? I was the theoretician, only I: he, although the proprietor of the lab (to a certain degree, and then only at second hand), indeed, precisely because he was in a position to boast of other qualities, should have abstained from criticism. "Now we shall see," I said: I carefully lifted the cathode jar and, holding it with its open end down, lit a match and brought it close. There was an explosion, small but sharp and angry, the jar burst into splinters (luckily, I was holding it level with my chest and not higher), and there remained in my hand, as a sarcastic symbol, the glass ring of the bottom.

We left, discussing what had occurred. My legs were shaking

a bit; I experienced retrospective fear and at the same time a kind of foolish pride, at having confirmed a hypothesis and having unleashed a force of nature. It was indeed hydrogen, therefore: the same element that burns in the sun and stars, and from whose condensation the universes are formed in eternal silence.

ZINC

For five months we had attended, packed together like sardines
and full of reverence, Professor P.'s classes in General and
Inorganic Chemistry, carrying away from them varied sensations, but all of them exciting and new. No, P.'s chemistry was
not the motor-force of the Universe, nor the key to the Truth:
P. was a skeptical, ironic old man, the enemy of all forms of
rhetoric (for this reason, and only for this, he was an anti-
Fascist), intelligent, obstinate, and quick-witted with a sad sort
of wit.

His students handed down stories of his examinations conducted with ferocious coldness and ostentatious prejudice: his
favorite victims were women in general, and then nuns, priests,
and all those who appeared before him "dressed like soldiers."   *29*

On his account were whispered murky legends of maniacal stinginess in running the Chemical Institute and his personal laboratory: that he conserved in the basements innumerable boxes of used matches, which he forbade the beadles to throw away; and that the mysterious minarets of the Institute itself, which even now confer on that section of the Corso Massimo d'Azeglio a jejune tone of fake exoticism, had been built at his bidding, in his remote youth, in order to celebrate there each year a foul and secret orgy of salvage. During it all the past year's rags and filter papers were burnt, and he personally analyzed the ashes with beggarly patience to extract from them all the valuable elements (and perhaps even less valuable) in a kind of ritual palingenesis which only Caselli, his faithful technician-beadle, was authorized to attend. It was also said that he had spent his entire academic career demolishing a certain theory of stereo-chemistry, not with experiments but with publications. The experiments were performed by someone else, his great rival, in some unknown part of the world; as he proceeded, the reports appeared in the *Helvetica Chemica Acta*, and Professor P. tore them apart one by one.

I could not swear to the authenticity of these rumors: but in fact, when he came into the laboratory for Preparations, no Bunsen burner was even low enough, so it was prudent to turn it off completely; actually, he made the students prepare silver nitrate from the five-lire coins taken from their own pockets, and chloride of nickel from the twenty-cent pieces with the flying naked lady; and in truth, the only time I was admitted to his study, I found written on the blackboard in a fine script: "Don't give me a funeral, neither dead nor alive."

I liked P. I liked the sober rigor of his classes; I was amused by the disdainful ostentation with which at the exams he exhibited, instead of the prescribed Fascist shirt, a comic black bib no bigger than the palm of a hand, which at each of his brusque movements would pop out between his jacket's lapels. I valued his two textbooks, clear to the point of obsession, concise, saturated with his surly contempt for humanity in general and for lazy and foolish students in particular: for all students were, by definition, lazy and foolish; anyone who by rare good luck managed to prove that he was not became his peer and was honored by a laconic and precious sentence of praise.

Now the five months of anxious waiting had passed: from among us eighty freshmen had been selected the twenty least lazy and foolish—fourteen boys and six girls—and the Preparation laboratory opened its doors to us. None of us had a precise idea of what was at stake: I think that it was his invention, a modern and technical version of the initiation rituals of savages, in which each of his subjects was abruptly torn away from book and school bench and transplanted amid eye-smarting fumes, hand-scorching acids, and practical events that do not jibe with the theories. I certainly do not want to dispute the usefulness, indeed the necessity of this initiation: but in the brutality with which it was carried out it was easy to see P.'s spiteful talent, his vocation for hierarchical distances and the humiliation of us, his flock. In sum: not a word, spoken or written, was spent by him as viaticum, to encourage us along the road we had chosen, to point out the dangers and pitfalls, and to communicate to us the tricks of the trade. I have often thought that deep down P. was a savage, a hunter; someone who goes hunting simply has to take along a gun, in fact a bow and arrow, and go into the woods: success or failure are purely up to him. Pick up and go, when the time comes the haruspices and augurs no longer count, theory is useless and you learn along the way, the experiences of others are useless, the essential is to meet the challenge. He who is worthy wins; he who has weak eyes, arms, or instincts turns back and changes his trade: of the eighty students I mentioned, thirty changed their trade in their second year and another twenty later on.

That laboratory was tidy and clean. We stayed in it five hours a day, from two o'clock to seven o'clock: at the entrance, an assistant assigned to each student a preparation, then each of us went to the supply room, where the hirsute Caselli handed out the raw material, foreign or domestic: a chunk of marble to this fellow, ten grams of bromine to the next, a bit of boric acid to another, a handful of clay to yet another. Caselli would entrust these reliquiae to us with an undisguised air of suspicion: this was the bread of science, P.'s bread, and finally it was also the stuff that he administered; who knows what improper use we profane and unskilled persons would make of it?

Caselli loved P. with a bitter, polemical love. Apparently he had been faithful to him for forty years; he was his shadow, his earthbound incarnation, and, like all those who perform vicarial functions, he was an interesting human specimen: like those, I mean to say, who represent Authority without possessing any of their own, such as, for example, sacristans, museum guides, beadles, nurses, the "young men" working for lawyers and notaries, and salesmen. These people, to a greater or lesser degree, tend to transfuse the human substance of their chief into their own mold, as occurs with pseudomorphic crystals: sometimes they suffer from it, often they enjoy it, and they possess two distinct patterns of behavior, depending on whether they act on their own or "in the exercise of their function." It often happens that the personality of their chief invades them so completely as to disturb their normal human contacts and so they remain celibate: celibacy is in fact prescribed and accepted in the monastic state, which entails precisely the proximity and subjection to the highest authority. Caselli was a modest, taciturn man, in whose sad but proud eyes could be read:

—he is a great scientist, and as his "famulus" I also am a little great;

—I, though humble, know things that he does not know;

—I know him better than he knows himself; I foresee his acts;

—I have power over him; I defend and protect him;

—I can say bad things about him because I love him; that is not granted to you;

—his principles are right, but he applies them laxly, and
"once upon a time it was not like this." If I weren't here . . . and

in fact, Caselli ran the Institute with a parsimony and hatred of novelty even greater than P.'s.

The first day it was my fate to be assigned the preparation of zinc sulfate: it should not have been too difficult; it was a matter of making an elementary stoichiometric calculation and attacking the zinc particles with previously diluted sulfuric acid: concentrate, crystallize, dry with the pump, wash and recrystallize. Zinc, Zinck, zinco: they make tubs out of it for laundry, it is not an element which says much to the imagination, it is gray and its salts are colorless, it is not toxic, nor does it produce striking chromatic reactions; in short, it is a boring metal. It has been known to humanity for two or three centuries, so it is not a veteran covered with glory like copper, nor even one of those newly minted elements which are still surrounded with the glamour of their discovery.

Caselli handed me my zinc; I returned to the bench and prepared to work: I felt curious, shy, and vaguely annoyed, as when you reach thirteen and must go to the temple to recite in Hebrew the Bar Mitzvah prayer before the rabbi; the moment, desired and somewhat feared, had come. The hour of the appointment with Matter, the Spirit's great antagonist, had struck: *hyle*, which, strangely, can be found embalmed in the endings of alkyl radicals: methyl, butyl, etc.

There was no need to get from Caselli the other raw material, the partner of zinc, that is, sulfuric acid: it was there in abundance in every corner. Concentrated, of course: and you had to dilute it with water; but watch out! it is written in all the treatises, one must operate in reverse, that is, pour the acid in the water and not the other way around, otherwise that innocuous-looking oil is prone to wild rages: this is known even to the kids in *liceo*. Then you put the zinc in the diluted acid.

The course notes contained a detail which at first reading had escaped me, namely, that the so tender and delicate zinc, so yielding to acid which gulps it down in a single mouthful, behaves, however, in a very different fashion when it is very pure: then it obstinately resists the attack. One could draw from this two conflicting philosophical conclusions: the praise of purity, which protects from evil like a coat of mail; the praise of impurity, which gives rise to changes, in other words, to life. I discarded the first, disgustingly moralistic, and I lingered to consider the second, which I found more congenial. In order for the wheel to turn, for life to be lived, impurities are needed, and the impurities of impurities in the soil, too, as is known, if it is to be fertile. Dissension, diversity, the grain of salt and mustard are needed: Fascism does not want them, forbids them, and that's why you're not a Fascist; it wants everybody to be the same, and you are not. But immaculate virtue does not exist either, or if it exists it is detestable. So take the solution of copper sulfate which is in the shelf of reagents, add a drop of it to your sulfuric acid, and you'll see the reaction begin: the zinc wakes up, it is covered with a white fur of hydrogen bubbles, and there we are, the enchantment has taken place, you can leave it to its fate and take a stroll around the lab and see what's new and what the others are doing.

The others are doing various things: some are working intently, perhaps whistling to give themselves a nonchalant air, each one behind his particle of *hyle*; others are roaming about or gazing out the windows at Valentino Park, by now entirely green; still others are smoking and chatting in the corners.

In one corner there was a hood, and Rita sat in front of it. I went over to her and realized with fleeting pleasure that she was cooking my same dish: with pleasure, I say, because for some time now I had been hanging around Rita, mentally preparing brilliant conversational openings, and then at the decisive moment I did not dare come out with them and put it off to the next day. I did not dare because of my deep-rooted shyness and lack of confidence, and also because Rita discouraged all contact, it was hard to understand why. She was very thin, pale, sad, and sure of herself: she got through the exams with good marks, but without the genuine appetite that I felt for the things she had to study. She was nobody's friend, no one knew anything about her, she said very little, and for all these reasons she attracted me; I tried to sit next to her in class and she did not take me into her confidence, and I felt frustrated and challenged. In fact I was desperate, and surely not for the first time; actually at that period I thought myself condemned to a perpetual masculine solitude, denied a woman's smile forever, which I nevertheless needed as much as air.

It was quite clear that on that day I was being presented with an opportunity that should not be wasted: at that moment between Rita and myself there was a bridge, a small zinc bridge, fragile but negotiable; come on now, take the first step.

Buzzing around Rita, I became aware of a second fortunate circumstance: a familiar book jacket, yellowish with a red border, stuck out of the girl's bag; the image was a raven with a book in its beak. The title? You could read only IC and TAIN, but that's all I needed: it was my sustenance during those months, the timeless story of Hans Castorp in enchanted exile on the magic mountain. I asked Rita about it, on tenterhooks to hear her opinion, as if I had written the book: and soon enough I had to realize that she was reading the novel in an entirely different way. As a novel, in fact: she was very interested in finding out exactly how far Hans would go with Madame Chauchat, and mercilessly skipped the fascinating (for me) political, theological, and metaphysical discussions between the humanist Settembrini and the Jewish Jesuit Naphtha.

Never mind: actually, it's ground for debate. It could even become an essential and fundamental discussion, because I too am Jewish, and she is not: I am the impurity that makes the zinc react, I am the grain of salt or mustard. Impurity, certainly, since just during those months the publication of the magazine *Defense of the Race* had begun, and there was much talk about purity, and I had begun to be proud of being impure. In truth, until precisely those months it had not meant much to me that I was a Jew: within myself, and in my contacts with my Christian friends, I had always considered my origin as an almost negligible but curious fact, a small amusing anomaly, like having a crooked nose or freckles; a Jew is somebody who at Christmas does not have a tree, who should not eat salami but eats it all the same, who has learned a bit of Hebrew at thirteen and then has forgotten it. According to the above-mentioned magazine, a Jew is stingy and cunning; but I was not particularly stingy or cunning, nor had my father been.

So there was plenty to discuss with Rita, but the conversation I had in mind didn't strike a spark. I soon realized that Rita was different from me: she was not a grain of mustard; she was the daughter of a poor, sickly storekeeper. For her the university was not at all the temple of Knowledge: it was a thorny and difficult path which led to a degree, a job, and regular pay. She herself had worked since childhood: she had helped her father, had been a salesgirl in a village store, and had also ridden about Turin on a bicycle, making deliveries and picking up payments. All this did not put a distance between us; on the contrary I found it admirable, like everything that was part of her: her not very well cared for, rough-looking hands, her modest dress, her steady gaze, her concrete sadness, the reserve with which she accepted my remarks.

So my zinc sulfate ended up badly by concentrating, turned into nothing more than a bit of white powder which in suffocating clouds exhaled all or almost all of its sulfuric acid. I left it to its fate and asked Rita to let me walk her home. It was dark, and her home was not close by. The goal that I had set myself was objectively modest, but it seemed to me incomparably audacious: I hesitated half of the way and felt on burning coals, and intoxicated myself and her with disjointed, breathless talk. Finally, trembling with emotion, I slipped my arm under hers. Rita did not pull away, nor did she return the pressure: but I fell into step with her, and felt exhilarated and victorious. It seemed to me that I had won a small but decisive battle against the darkness, the emptiness, and the hostile years that lay ahead.

IRON

Night lay beyond the walls of the Chemical Institute, the night of Europe: Chamberlain had returned from Munich duped, Hitler had marched into Prague without firing a shot, Franco had subdued Barcelona and was ensconced in Madrid. Fascist Italy, the small-time pirate, had occupied Albania, and the premonition of imminent catastrophe condensed like grumous dew in the houses and streets, in wary conversations and dozing consciences.

But the night did not penetrate those thick walls; Fascist censorship itself, the regime's masterwork, kept us shut off from the world, in a white, anesthetized limbo. About thirty of us had managed to surmount the harsh barrier of the first exams and had been admitted to the second year's Qualitative Analysis 37 laboratory. We had entered that enormous, dark, smoky hall like someone who, coming into the House of the Lord, reflects on each of his steps. The previous lab, where I had tackled zinc, seemed an infantile exercise to us now, similar to when as children we had played at cooking: something, by hook or crook, in one way or another, always came of it, perhaps too little, perhaps not very pure, but you really had to be a hopeless case or pigheaded not to get magnesium sulfate from magnesite, or potassium bromide from bromine.

Not here: here the affair had turned serious, the confrontation with Mother-Matter, our hostile mother, was tougher and closer. At two in the afternoon, Professor D., with his ascetic and distracted air, handed each of us precisely one gram of a certain powder: by the next day we had to complete the qualitative analysis, that is, report what metals and non-metals it contained. Report in writing, like a police report, only yes and no, because doubts and hesitations were not admissible: it was each time a choice, a deliberation, a mature and responsible undertaking, for which Fascism had not prepared us, and from which emanated a good smell, dry and clean.

Some elements, such as iron and copper, were easy and direct, incapable of concealment; others, such as bismuth and cadmium, were deceptive and elusive. There was a method, a toilsome, age-old plan for systematic research, a kind of combined steamroller and fine-toothed comb which nothing (in theory) could escape, but I preferred to invent each time a new road, with swift, extemporaneous forays, as in a war of movement, instead of the deadly grind of a war of position. Sublimate mercury into droplets, transform sodium into chloride, and identify it as trough-shaped chips under my microscope. One way or another, here the relationship with Matter changed, became dialectical: it was fencing, a face-to-face match. Two unequal opponents: on one side, putting the questions, the unfledged, unarmed chemist, at his elbow the textbook by Autenrieth as his sole ally (because D., often called to help out in difficult cases, maintained a scrupulous neutrality, refused to give an opinion: a wise attitude, since whoever opens his mouth can put his foot in it, and professors are not supposed to do that); on the other side, responding with enigmas, stood Matter, with her sly passivity, ancient as the All and portentously rich in deceptions, as solemn and subtle as the Sphinx. I was just beginning to read German words and was enchanted by the word *Urstoff* (which means "element": literally, "primal substance") and by the prefix *Ur* which appeared in it and which in fact expresses ancient origin, remote distance in space and time.

In this place, too, nobody wasted many words teaching us how to protect ourselves from acids, caustics, fires, and explosions; it appeared that the Institute's rough and ready morality counted on the process of natural selection to pick out those among us most qualified for physical and professional survival. There were few ventilation hoods; each student, following his text's prescriptions, in the course of systematic analysis, conscientiously let loose into the air a good dose of hydrochloric acid and ammonia, so that a dense, hoary mist of ammonium chloride stagnated permanently in the lab, depositing minute scintillating crystals on the windowpanes. Into the hydrogen sulfide room with its murderous atmosphere withdrew couples seeking privacy and a few lone wolves to eat their snacks.

Through the murk and in the busy silence, we heard a Piedmontese voice say: *"Nuntio vobis gaudium magnum. Habemus ferrum."* "I announce to you a great joy. We have iron." It was March 1939, and a few days earlier an almost identical solemn announcement (*"Habemus Papam"*) had closed the conclave that had raised to Peter's Throne Cardinal Eugenio Pacelli, in whom many put their hopes, since one must after all put one's hope in someone or something. The blasphemous announcement came from Sandro, the quiet one.

In our midst, Sandro was a loner. He was a boy of medium height, thin but muscular, who never wore an overcoat, even on the coldest days. He came to class in worn corduroy knickers, knee socks made of homespun wool and sometimes a short black cape which made me think of the Tuscan poet Renato

Fucini. He had large, calloused hands, a bony, rugged profile, a face baked by the sun, a low forehead beneath the line of his hair, which he wore very short and cut in a brush. He walked with the peasant's long, slow stride.

A few months before, the racial laws against the Jews had been proclaimed, and I too was becoming a loner. My Christian classmates were civil people; none of them, nor any of the teachers, had directed at me a hostile word or gesture, but I could feel them withdraw and, following an ancient pattern, I withdrew as well: every look exchanged between me and them was accompanied by a minuscule but perceptible flash of mistrust and suspicion. What do you think of me? What am I for you? The same as six months ago, your equal who does not go to Mass, or the Jew who, as Dante put it, "in your midst laughs at you"?

I had noticed with amazement and delight that something was happening between Sandro and me. It was not at all a friendship born from affinity; on the contrary, the difference in our origins made us rich in "exchangeable goods," like two merchants who meet after coming from remote and mutually unknown regions. Nor was it the normal, portentous intimacy of twenty-year-olds: with Sandro I never reached this point. I soon realized that he was generous, subtle, tenacious, and brave, even with a touch of insolence, but he had an elusive, untamed quality; so that, although we were at the age when one always has the need, instinct, and immodesty of inflicting on one another everything that swarms in one's head and elsewhere (and this is an age that can last long, but ends with the first compromise), nothing had gotten through his carapace of reserve, nothing of his inner world, which nevertheless one felt was dense and fertile—nothing save a few occasional, dramatically truncated hints. He had the nature of a cat with whom one can live for decades without ever being permitted to penetrate its sacred pelt.

We had many concessions to make to each other. I told him we were like cation and anion, but Sandro did not seem to acknowledge the comparison. He was born in Serra d'Ivrea, a beautiful but niggardly region. He was the son of a mason and spent his summers working as a shepherd. Not a shepherd of souls: a shepherd of sheep, and not because of Arcadian rhetoric or eccentricity, but happily, out of love for the earth and grass and an abundance of heart. He had a curious mimetic talent, and when he talked about cows, chickens, sheep, and dogs he was transformed, imitating their way of looking, their movements and voices, becoming very gay and seeming to turn into an animal himself, like a shaman. He taught me about plants and animals, but said very little about his family. His father had died when he was a child; they were simple, poor people, and since the boy was bright, they had decided to make him study so that he would bring money home: he had accepted this with Piedmontese seriousness but without enthusiasm. He had traveled the long route of high school—*liceo*—aiming at the highest marks with the least effort. He was not interested in Catullus and Descartes, he was interested in being promoted, and spending Sunday on his skis and climbing the rocks. He had chosen chemistry because he had thought it better than other studies; it was a trade that dealt with things one can see and touch, a way to earn one's bread less tiring than working as a carpenter or a peasant.

We began studying physics together, and Sandro was surprised when I tried to explain to him some of the ideas that at the time I was confusedly cultivating. That the nobility of Man, acquired in a hundred centuries of trial and error, lay in making himself the conqueror of matter, and that I had enrolled in chemistry because I wanted to remain faithful to this nobility. That conquering matter is to understand it, and understanding matter is necessary to understanding the universe and ourselves: and that therefore Mendeleev's Periodic Table, which just during those weeks we were laboriously learning to unravel, was poetry, loftier and more solemn than all the poetry we had swallowed down in liceo; and come to think of it, it even rhymed! That if one looked for the bridge, the missing link, between the world of words and the world of things, one did not have to look far: it was there, in our Autenrieth, in our smoke-filled labs, and in our future trade.

And finally, and fundamentally, an honest and open boy, did he not smell the stench of Fascist truths which tainted the sky? Did he not perceive it as an ignominy that a thinking man should be asked to believe without thinking? Was he not filled with disgust at all the dogmas, all the unproved affirmations, all the imperatives? He did feel it; so then, how could he not feel a new dignity and majesty in our study, how could he ignore the fact that the chemistry and physics on which we fed, besides being in themselves nourishments vital in themselves, were the antidote to Fascism which he and I were seeking, because they were clear and distinct and verifiable at every step, and not a tissue of lies and emptiness, like the radio and newspapers?

Sandro listened to me with ironical attention, always ready to deflate me with a couple of civil and terse words when I trespassed into rhetoric. But something was ripening in him (certainly not all my doing; those were months heavy with fateful events), something that troubled him because it was at once new and ancient. He, who until then had read only Salgari, Jack London, and Kipling, overnight became a furious reader: he digested and remembered everything, and everything in him spontaneously fell into place as a way of life; together with this, he began to study, and his average shot up from C to A. At the same time, out of unconscious gratitude, and perhaps also out of a desire to get even, he in turn took an interest in my education and made it clear to me that it had gaps. I might even be right: it might be that Matter is our teacher and perhaps also, for lack of something better, our political school; but he had another form of matter to lead me to, another teacher: not the powders of the Analytical Lab but the true, authentic, timeless *Urstoff*, the rocks and ice of the nearby mountains. He proved to me without too much difficulty that I didn't have the proper credentials to talk about matter. What commerce, what intimacy had I had, until then, with Empedocles' four elements? Did I know how to light a stove? Wade across a torrent? Was I familiar with a storm high up in the mountains? The sprouting of seeds? No. So he too had something vital to teach me.

A comradeship was born, and there began for me a feverish season. Sandro seemed to be made of iron, and he was bound to iron by an ancient kinship: his father's fathers, he told me, had been tinkers (*magnín*) and blacksmiths in the Canavese valleys: they made nails on the charcoal forges, sheathed wagon wheels with red-hot hoops, pounded iron plates until deafened by the noise; and he himself when he saw the red vein of iron in the rock felt he was meeting a friend. In the winter when it suddenly hit him, he would tie his skis on his rusty bike, leaving early in the morning and pedaling away until he reached the snow, without a cent, an artichoke in one pocket and the other full of lettuce; then he came back in the evening or even the next day, sleeping in haylofts, and the more storms and hunger he suffered the happier and healthier he was.

In the summer, when he went off by himself, he often took along a dog to keep him company. This was a small yellow mongrel with a downcast expression; in fact, as Sandro had told me, acting out in his way the animal episode, as a puppy he had had a mishap with a cat. He had come too close to a litter of newborn kittens, the mother cat was miffed and became enraged, and had begun to hiss, getting all puffed up; but the puppy had not yet learned the meaning of those signals and remained there like a fool. The cat had attacked him, chased him, caught him, and scratched his nose; the dog had been permanently traumatized. He felt dishonored, and so Sandro had made him a cloth ball, explained to him that it was the cat, and every morning presented it to him so that he could take his revenge on it for the insult and regain his canine honor. For the same therapeutic motive, Sandro took him to the mountains, so he could have some fun: he tied him to one end of a rope, tied himself to the other, set the dog firmly on a rock ledge, and then climbed up; when the rope ended, he pulled it up slowly, and the dog had learned to walk up with his muzzle pointed skywards and his four paws against the nearly vertical wall of rock, moaning softly as though he were dreaming.

Sandro climbed the rocks more by instinct than technique, trusting to the strength of his hands and saluting ironically, in the projecting rock to which he clung, the silicon, calcium, and magnesium he had learned to recognize in the course on mineralogy. He seemed to feel that he had wasted a day if he had not in some way gotten to the bottom of his reserve of energy, and then even his eyes became brighter and he explained to me that, with a sedentary life, a deposit of fat forms behind the eyes, which is not healthy; by working hard the fat is consumed and the eyes sink back into their sockets and become keener.

He spoke grudgingly about his exploits. He did not belong to that species of persons who do things in order to talk about them (like me); he did not like high-sounding words, indeed words. It appeared that in speaking, as in mountain climbing, he had never received lessons; he spoke as no one speaks, saying only the core of things.

If necessary he carried a thirty-kilo pack, but usually he traveled without it; his pockets were sufficient, and in them he put some vegetables, as I have said, a chunk of bread, a pocketknife, sometimes the dog-eared Alpine Club guide, and a skein of wire for emergency repairs. In fact he did not carry the guide because he believed in it, but for the opposite reason. He rejected it because he felt that it shackled him; not only that, he also saw it as a bastard creature, a detestable hybrid of snow and rock mixed up with paper. He took it into the mountains to vilify. Happy if he could catch it in an error, even if it was at his and his climbing companion's expense. He could walk for two days without eating, or eat three meals all together and then leave. For him, all seasons were good. In the winter he skied, but not at the well-equipped, fashionable slopes, which he shunned with laconic scorn: too poor to buy ourselves the sealskin strips for the ascents, he showed me how you sew on rough hemp cloths, Spartan devices which absorb the water and then freeze like codfish, and must be tied around your waist when you ski downhill. He dragged me along on exhausting treks through the fresh snow, far from any sign of human life, following routes that he seemed to intuit like a savage. In the summer, from shelter to shelter, inebriating ourselves with the sun, the effort, and the wind, and scraping the skin of our fingertips on rocks never before touched by human hands: but not on the famous peaks, nor in quest of memorable feats; such things did not matter to him at all. What mattered was to know his limitations, to test and improve himself; more obscurely, he felt the need to prepare himself (and to prepare me) for an iron future, drawing closer month by month.

To see Sandro in the mountains reconciled you to the world and made you forget the nightmare weighing on Europe. This was his place, what he had been made for, like the marmots whose whistle and snout he imitated: in the mountains he became happy, with a silent, infectious happiness, like a light that is switched on. He aroused a new communion with the earth and sky, into which flowed my need for freedom, the plenitude of my strength, and a hunger to understand the things he had pushed me toward. We would come out at dawn, rubbing our eyes, through the small door of the Martinotti bivouac, and there, all around us, barely touched by the sun, stood the white and brown mountains, new as if created during the night that had just ended and at the same time innumerably ancient. They were an island, an elsewhere.

In any event, it was not always necessary to go high and far. In the in-between seasons Sandro's kingdom was the rock gymnasiums. There are several, two or three hours by bike from Turin, and I would be curious to know whether they are still frequented: the Straw Stack Pinnacles with the Wolkmann Tower, the Teeth of Cumiana, Patanüa Rock (which means Bare Rock), the Plô, the Sbarüa, and others, with their homely, modest names. The last, the Sbarüa, I think was discovered by Sandro himself and a mythical brother of his whom Sandro never let me see but who, from his few scanty   *45* hints, must have stood in the same relationship to him as he stood to the run of humanity. Sbarüa is a noun from the verb sbarüé, which means "to terrify"; the Sbarüa is a prism of granite that towers about a hundred meters above a modest hill bristling with brambles and a brushwood coppice; like Dante's Veglio di Creta—the Old Man of Crete—it is split from base to summit by a fissure that gets narrower as it rises, finally forcing the climber to come out on the rock face itself, where, precisely, he is terrified, and where at that time there was just a single piton, charitably left behind by Sandro's brother.

Those were curious places, frequented by a few dozen amateurs of our stamp, all of whom Sandro knew either by name or sight: we climbed up, not without technical problems, and surrounded by the irritating buzz of enormous bluebottle flies attracted by our sweat, crawling up good solid rock walls interrupted by grassy ledges where ferns and strawberries grew or, in the fall, blackberries: often enough we used as holds the trunks of puny little trees, rooted in the cracks, and after a few hours we reached the peak, which was not a peak at all but mostly placid pastureland where cows stared at us with indifferent eyes. Then we descended at breakneck speed, in a few minutes, along paths strewn with old and recent cow dung, to recover our bikes.

At other times our exploits were more demanding; never any quiet jaunts, since Sandro said that we would have plenty of time when we were forty to look at the scenery. "Let's go, shall we?" he said to me one day in February—which in his language meant that, since the weather was good, we should leave in the afternoon for the winter climb of the Tooth of M., which for some weeks had been one of our projects. We slept in an inn and left the next day, not too early, at some undetermined hour (Sandro did not like watches: he felt their quiet continuous admonishment to be an arbitrary intrusion). We plunged boldly into the fog and came out of it about one o'clock, in gleaming sunlight and on the big crest of a peak which was not the right one.

I then said that we should be able to go down about a hundred meters, cross over halfway up the mountain, and go up along the next ridge: or, better yet, since we were already there, continue climbing and be satisfied with the wrong peak, which in any case was only forty meters lower than the right one. But Sandro, with splendid bad faith, said in a few dense syllables that my last proposal was fine, but from there "by way of the easy northwest ridge" (this was a sarcastic quotation from the abovementioned Alpine Club guide) we could also reach the Tooth of M. in half an hour; and what was the point of being twenty if you couldn't permit yourself the luxury of taking the wrong route.

The easy ridge must really have been easy, indeed elementary in the summer; but we found it in a very discomforting state. The rock was wet on the side facing the sun and covered with a black layer of ice in the shade; between one large outcrop of rock and another lay pockets of melting snow into which we sank to our waists. We reached the top at five; I dragged myself along so pitifully that it was painful, while Sandro was seized by a sinister hilarity that I found very annoying.

"And how do we get down?"

"As for getting down, we shall see," he replied, and added mysteriously: "The worst that can happen is to have to taste bear meat." Well, we tasted bear meat in the course of that night, which seemed very, very long. We got down in two hours, helped badly by the rope, which was frozen; it had become a malignant, rigid tangle that snagged on each projection and rang against the rock face like the cable of a funicular. At seven we were on the bank of a frozen pond and it was dark. We ate the little that was left, built a useless dry stone wall facing the wind, and lay down on the ground to sleep, pressed to each other. It was as though time itself had frozen; every so often we got to our feet to reactivate our circulation, and it was always the same time: the wind never stopped blowing, there was always the same ghost of a moon, always at the same point in the sky, and in front of the moon passed a fantastic cavalcade of tattered clouds, always the same. We had taken off our shoes, as described in Lammer's books, so dear to Sandro, and we kept our feet in our packs; at the first funereal light, which seemed to seep from the snow and not the sky, we rose with our limbs benumbed and our eyes glittering from lack of sleep, hunger, and the hardness of our bed. And we found our shoes so frozen that they rang like bells, and to get them on we had to hatch them out like brood hens.

But we went back down to the valley under our own steam; and to the innkeeper who asked us, with a snicker, how things had gone, and meanwhile was staring at our wild, exalted faces, we answered flippantly that we had had an excellent outing, then paid the bill and departed with dignity. This was it—the bear meat; and now that many years have passed, I regret that I ate so little of it, for nothing has had, even distantly, the taste of that meat, which is the taste of being strong and free, free also to make mistakes and be the master of one's destiny. That is why I am grateful to Sandro for having led me consciously into trouble, on that trip and other undertakings which were only apparently foolish, and I am certain that they helped me later on.

They didn't help Sandro, or not for long. Sandro was Sandro Delmastro, the first man to be killed fighting in the Resistance with the Action Party's Piedmontese Military Command. After a few months of extreme tension, in April of 1944 he was captured by the Fascists, did not surrender, and tried to escape from the Fascist Party house in Cuneo. He was killed with a tommygun burst in the back of the neck by a monstrous child-executioner, one of those wretched murderers of fifteen whom Mussolini's Republic of Salò recruited in the reformatories. His body was abandoned in the road for a long time, because the Fascists had forbidden the population to bury him.

Today I know that it is a hopeless task to try to dress a man in words, make him live again on the printed page, especially a man like Sandro. He was not the sort of person you can tell stories about, nor to whom one erects monuments—he who laughed at all monuments: he lived completely in his deeds, and when they were over nothing of him remains—nothing but words, precisely.

POTASSIUM

In January 1941 the fate of Europe and the world seemed to be sealed. Only the deluded could still think that Germany would not win; the stolid English "had not noticed that they had lost the game," and obstinately resisted under the bombings; but they were alone and suffered bloody losses on all fronts. Only a voluntarily deaf and blind man could have any doubts about the fate reserved for the Jews in a German Europe: we had read Feuchtwanger's *Oppermanns*, smuggled secretly in from France, and a British White Book, which arrived from Palestine and described the "Nazi atrocities"; we had only believed half of it, but that was enough. Many refugees from Poland and France had reached Italy, and we had talked with them: they did not know the details of the slaughters that were taking place behind a monstrous curtain of silence, but each of them was a messenger, like those who run to Job to tell him, "I alone have escaped to tell you the story."

And yet, if we wanted to live, if we wished in some way to take advantage of the youth coursing through our veins, there was indeed no other resource than self-imposed blindness; like the English, "we did not notice," we pushed all dangers into the limbo of things not perceived or immediately forgotten. We could also, in the abstract, throw everything away and escape and be transplanted to some remote, mythical country, chosen from among the few that kept their frontiers open: Madagascar, British Honduras. But to do this one needed a lot of money and a fabulous capacity for initiative—and I, my family, and our friends had neither one nor the other. Besides, if looked at from close by and in detail, things did not after all seem so disastrous: the Italy around us, or, to put it more accurately (at a time when one traveled little), Piedmont and Turin were not hostile. Piedmont was our true country, the one in which we recognized ourselves; the mountains around Turin, visible on clear days, and within reach of a bicycle, were ours, irreplaceable, and had taught us fatigue, endurance, and a certain wisdom. In short, our roots were in Piedmont and Turin, not enormous but deep, extensive, and fantastically intertwined.

Neither in us nor, more generally, in our generation, whether "Aryan" or Jew, had the idea yet gained ground that one must and could resist Fascism. Our resistance at the time was passive and was limited to rejection, isolation, and avoiding contamination. The seed of active struggle had not survived down to us, it had been stifled a few years before with the final sweep of the scythe, which had relegated to prison, house arrest, exile, or silence the last Turinese protagonists and witnesses—Einaudi, Ginzburg, Monti, Vittorio Foa, Zini, Carlo Levi. These names said nothing to us, we knew hardly anything about them—the Fascism around us did not have opponents. We had to begin from scratch, "invent" our anti-Fascism, create it from the germ, from the roots, from our roots. We looked around us and traveled up roads that led not very far away. The Bible, Croce, geometry, and physics seemed to us sources of certainty.

We gathered in the gym of the Talmud Torah—in the School of the Law, as the very old Hebrew elementary school was proudly called—and taught each other to find again in the Bible justice and injustice and the strength that overcomes injustice; to recognize the new oppressors in Ahasuerus and Nebuchadnezzar. But where was Kadosh Barukhú, "the Holy One, Blessed be He": he who breaks the slaves' chains and submerges the Egyptians' chariots? He who dictated the Law to Moses, and inspired the liberators Ezra and Nehemiah, no longer inspired anyone; the sky above us was silent and empty: he allowed the Polish ghettos to be exterminated, and slowly, confusedly, the idea was making headway in us that we were alone, that we had no allies we could count on, neither on earth nor in heaven, that we would have to find in ourselves the strength to resist. Therefore the impulse that drove us to explore our limits was not completely absurd: to travel hundreds of kilometers on our bikes, to climb with fury and patience up rock walls that we did not know very well, to subject ourselves voluntarily to hunger, cold, and fatigue, to train ourselves to endure and to make decisions. A piton goes in or it doesn't; the rope holds or it doesn't: these too were sources of certainty.

Chemistry, for me, had stopped being such a source. It led to the heart of Matter, and Matter was our ally precisely because the Spirit, dear to Fascism, was our enemy; but, having reached the fourth year of Pure Chemistry, I could no longer ignore the fact that chemistry itself, or at least that which we were being administered, did not answer my questions. To prepare phenyl bromide or methyl violet according to Gattermann was amusing, even exhilarating, but not very much different from following Artusi's recipes. Why in that particular way and not in another? After having been force fed in *liceo* the truths revealed by Fascist Doctrine, all revealed, unproven truths either bored me stiff or aroused my suspicion. Did chemistry theorems exist? No: therefore you had to go further, not be satisfied with the *quia*, go back to the origins, to mathematics and physics. The origins of chemistry were ignoble, or at least equivocal: the dens of the alchemists, their abominable hodgepodge of ideas and language, their confessed interest in gold, their Levantine swindles typical of charlatans or magicians; instead, at the origin of physics lay the strenuous clarity of the West—Archimedes and Euclid. I would become a physicist, *ruat coelum*: perhaps without a degree, since Hitler and Mussolini forbade it.

A brief course of exercises in physics formed part of the fourth-year chemistry program: simple measurements of viscosity, surface tension, rotatory power, and suchlike exercises. The course was conducted by a young assistant, thin, tall, a bit hunched over, polite, and extraordinarily shy, who behaved in a way that we were not used to. Our other teachers, almost without exception, showed themselves convinced of the importance and excellence of the subject they taught; some of them were in good faith, for others it was evidently a matter of personal supremacy, of their private hunting grounds. That assistant, however, almost had the air of apologizing to us, of ranging himself on our side: in his somewhat embarrassed and well-bred ironic smile, one seemed to read: "I too know that with this antiquated and worn-out equipment you'll not be able to put together anything useful, and that furthermore these are all marginal futilities, and knowledge lives elsewhere; but this is a trade that you and I too must work at—so please try not to do much damage and to learn as much as you can." In short, all the girls in the course fell in love with him.

During the span of those months I made desperate attempts to be taken on as a student assistant by this or that professor. Some of them snidely or even arrogantly told me that the racial laws prohibited it; others fell back on hazy or flimsy excuses. After having imperturbably collected the fourth or fifth rejection, I was going home one evening on my bike, with an almost palpable load of disheartenment and bitterness on my back. I was pedaling listlessly up Via Valperga Caluso, while from the Valentino Park gusts of freezing wind overtook and passed me;

it was night by now, and the light of the street lamps, covered with purple for the blackout, did not prevail over the mist and darkness. The passersby were few and hurried; and then suddenly one among them caught my attention. He was going in my direction with a long, slow stride, he wore a long black overcoat, and his head was bare. He was walking a bit hunched over and looked like the assistant—it was the assistant. I passed him, uncertain as to what I should do; then I plucked up my courage, went back, and once again did not dare speak to him. What did I know about him? Nothing. He could be indifferent, a hypocrite, even an enemy. Then I thought that I risked nothing but another rejection, and without beating around the bush I asked him whether it would be possible to be accepted for experimental work in his school. The assistant looked at me with surprise; and instead of going into the long explanation I expected, he replied with two words from the Gospel: "Follow me."

The inside of the Institute of Experimental Physics was full of dust and century-old ghosts. There were rows of glass-doored cupboards packed with slips of paper, yellowed and gnawed by mice and paper moths: these were the observations of eclipses, registrations of earthquakes, meteorological bulletins from well into the last century. Along the walls of one corridor I found an extraordinary trumpet, more than thirty feet long, whose origin, purpose, and use no one any longer knew—perhaps it was to announce the Day of Judgment, when all that which is hidden will appear. There was an Aeolipyle in Secession style, a Hero's fountain, and a whole obsolete and prolix fauna of contraptions for generations destined for classroom demonstrations: a pathetic and ingenuous form of minor physics, in which stage setting counts for more than concept. It is neither illusionism nor conjuring trick but borders on them.

The assistant welcomed me in the tiny room on the ground floor where he himself lived, and which was bristling with a much different sort of equipment, unknown and exciting enthusiasm. Some molecules are carriers of an electrical dipole; they behave in short in an electrical field like minuscule compass needles: they orient themselves, some more sluggishly, others less so. Depending on conditions, they obey certain laws with greater or less respect. Well, now, these devices served to clarify those conditions and that inadequate respect. They were waiting for someone to put them to use; he was busy with other matters (astrophysics, he specified, and the information shook me to the marrow: so I had an astrophysicist right in front of me, in flesh and blood!) and besides he had no experience with certain manipulations which were considered necessary to purify the products that had to be measured; for this a chemist was necessary, and I was the welcomed chemist. He willingly handed over the field to me and the instruments. The field was two square meters of a table and desk; the instruments, a small family, but the most important were the Westphal balance and the heterodyne. The first I already knew; with the second I soon established a friendship. In substance it was a radio-receiving apparatus, built to reveal the slightest differences in frequency; and in fact, it went howlingly out of tune and barked like a watchdog simply if the operator shifted in his chair or moved a hand, or if someone just came into the room. Besides, at certain hours of the day, it revealed a whole intricate universe of mysterious messages, Morse tickings, modulated hisses, and deformed, mangled human voices, which pronounced sentences in incomprehensible languages, or others in Italian, but they were senseless sentences, in code. It was the radiophonic Babel of the war, messages of death transmitted by ships or planes from God knows who to God knows whom, beyond the mountains and the sea.

Beyond the mountains and the sea, the assistant explained to me, there was a scholar named Onsager, about whom he knew nothing except that he had worked out an equation that claimed to describe the behavior of polar molecules under all conditions, provided that they were in a liquid state. The equation functioned well for diluted solutions; it did not appear that anyone   55 had bothered to verify it for concentrated solutions, pure polar liquids, and mixtures of the latter. This was the work that he proposed I do, to prepare a series of complex liquids and check if they obeyed Onsager's equation, which I accepted with indiscriminate enthusiasm. As a first step, I would have to do something he did not know how to do: at that time it was not easy to find pure products for analysis, and I was supposed to devote myself for a few weeks to purifying benzene, chlorobenzene, chlorophenols, aminophenols, toluidines, and more.

A few hours of contact were sufficient for the assistant's personality to become clearly defined. He was thirty, was recently married, came from Trieste but was of Greek origin, knew four languages, loved music, Huxley, Ibsen, Conrad, and Thomas Mann, the last so dear to me. He also loved physics, but he was suspicious of every activity that set itself a goal: therefore, he was nobly lazy and, naturally, detested Fascism.

His relationship to physics perplexed me. He did not hesitate to harpoon my last hippogriff, confirming quite explicitly that message about "marginal futility" which we had read in his eyes in the lab. Not only those humble exercises of ours but physics as a whole was marginal, by its nature, by vocation, insofar as it set itself the task of regulating the universe of appearances, whereas the truth, the reality, the intimate essence of things and man exist elsewhere, hidden behind a veil, or seven veils (I don't remember exactly). He was a physicist, more precisely an astrophysicist, diligent and eager but without illusions: the Truth lay beyond, inaccessible to our telescopes, accessible to the initiates. This was a long road which he was traveling with effort, wonderment, and profound joy. Physics was prose: elegant gymnastics for the mind, mirror of Creation, the key to man's dominion over the planet; but what is the stature of Creation, of man and the planet? His road was long and he had barely started up it, but I was his disciple: Did I want to follow him?

It was a terrifying request. To be the assistant's disciple was
for me an enjoyment of every minute, a never before experi-

enced bond, without shadows, rendered more intense by the certainty that the relationship was mutual: I, a Jew, excluded and made skeptical by recent upheavals, the enemy of violence but not yet caught up in the necessity of an opposed violence, I should be for him the ideal interlocutor, a white sheet on which any message could be inscribed.

I did not mount the new gigantic hippogriff which the assistant offered me. During those months the Germans destroyed Belgrade, broke the Greek resistance, invaded Crete from the air: that was the Truth, that was the Reality. There were no escape routes, or not for me. Better to remain on the Earth, playing with the dipoles for lack of anything better, purify benzene and prepare for an unknown but imminent and certainly tragic future. To purify benzene, then, under the conditions to which the war and the bombings had reduced the Institute was not an insignificant undertaking: the assistant declared that I had carte blanche, I could rummage everywhere from basement to attic, appropriate any instrument or product, but I could not buy anything, even he couldn't, it was a regime of absolute autarky.

In the basement I found a huge demijohn of technical benzene, at 95 percent purity, better than nothing, but the manuals prescribed rectifying it and then putting it through a final distillation in the presence of sodium, to free it from the last traces of humidity. To rectify means to distill by fractions, discarding the fractions that boil lower or higher than prescribed, and gathering the "heart," which must boil at a constant temperature: I found in the inexhaustible basement the necessary glassware, including one of those Vigreux distillation columns, as pretty as a piece of lace, the product of superhuman patience and ability on the part of the glass blower, but (be it said between us) of debatable efficiency; I made the double boiler with a small aluminum pot.

Distilling is beautiful. First of all, because it is a slow, philosophic, and silent occupation, which keeps you busy but gives you time to think of other things, somewhat like riding a 57 bike. Then, because it involves a metamorphosis from liquid to vapor (invisible), and from this once again to liquid; but in this double journey, up and down, purity is attained, an ambiguous and fascinating condition, which starts with chemistry and goes very far. And finally, when you set about distilling, you acquire the consciousness of repeating a ritual consecrated by the centuries, almost a religious act, in which from imperfect material you obtain the essence, the *usia*, the spirit, and in the first place alcohol, which gladdens the spirit and warms the heart. I took two good days to obtain a fraction of satisfying purity: for this operation, since I had to work with an open flame, I had voluntarily exiled myself to a small room on the second floor, deserted and empty and far from any human presence.

Now I had to distill a second time in the presence of sodium. Sodium is a degenerated metal: it is indeed a metal only in the chemical significance of the word, certainly not in that of everyday language. It is neither rigid nor elastic; rather it is soft like wax; it is not shiny or, better, it is shiny only if preserved with maniacal care, since otherwise it reacts in a few instants with air, covering itself with an ugly rough rind: with even greater rapidity it reacts with water, in which it floats (a metal that floats!), dancing frenetically and developing hydrogen. I ransacked the entrails of the Institute in vain: like Ariosto's Astolfo on the Moon I found dozens of labeled ampules, hundreds of abstruse compounds, other vague anonymous sediments apparently untouched for generations, but not a sign of sodium. Instead I found a small phial of potassium: potassium is sodium's twin, so I grabbed it and returned to my hermitage.

I put in the flask of benzene a lump of potassium, "as large as half a pea"—so said the manual—and diligently distilled the contents: toward the end of the operation I dutifully doused the flame, took apart the apparatus, let the small amount of liquid in the flask cool off a bit, and then with a long pointed stick skewered the "half pea" of potassium and lifted it out.

Potassium, as I said, is sodium's twin, but it reacts with air and water with even greater energy: it is known to everyone (and was known also to me) that in contact with water it not only develops hydrogen but also ignites. So I handled my "half pea" like a holy relic: I placed it on a piece of dry filter paper, wrapped it up in it, went down into the Institute's courtyard, dug out a tiny grave, and buried the little bedeviled corpse. I carefully tamped down the earth above it and went back up to my work.

I took the now empty flask, put it under a faucet, and turned on the water. I heard a rapid thump and from the neck of the flask came a flash of flame directed at the window that was next to the washbasin and the curtains around it caught fire. While I was stumbling around looking for some even primitive means to extinguish it, the panels of the shutter began to blister and the room was now full of smoke. I managed to push over a chair and tear down the curtains; I threw them on the floor and stomped furiously on them, while the smoke half blinded me and my blood was throbbing violently in my temples.

When it was all over, when the incandescent tatters were extinguished, I remained standing there for a few minutes, weak and stunned, my knees turned to water, contemplating the vestiges of the disaster without seeing them. As soon as I got my breath back, I went to the floor below and told the assistant what had happened. If it is true that there is no greater sorrow than to remember a happy time in a state of misery, it is just as true that calling up a moment of anguish in a tranquil mood, seated quietly at one's desk, is a source of profound satisfaction.

The assistant listened to my account with polite attention but with a questioning look: Who had compelled me to embark on that voyage, and to distill benzene by going to so much trouble? In a way, it served me right: these are the things that happen to the profane, to those who dawdle and play before the portals of the temple instead of going inside. But he didn't say a word; he resorted for the occasion (unwillingly, as always) to the hierarchical distance and pointed out to me that an empty flask does not catch fire: so it must not have been empty. It must have contained, if nothing else, the vapor of the benzene, besides of course the air that came in through its neck. But one has never seen the vapor of benzene, when cold, catch fire by itself: only the potassium could have set fire to the mixture, and I had taken out the potassium. All of it?

All, I answered; but then I was visited by a doubt, returned to the scene of the accident, and found fragments of the flask still on the floor: on one of them, by looking closely, one could see, barely visible, a tiny white fleck. I tested it with phenolphthalein: it was basic, it was potassium hydroxide. The guilty party had been found: adhering to the glass of the flask there must have remained a minuscule particle of potassium, all that was needed to react with the water I had poured in and set fire to the benzene vapors.

The assistant looked at me with an amused, vaguely ironic expression: better not to do than to do, better to meditate than to act, better his astrophysics, the threshold of the Unknowable, than my chemistry, a mess compounded of stenches, explosions, and small futile mysteries. I thought of another moral, more down to earth and concrete, and I believe that every militant chemist can confirm it: that one must distrust the almost-the-same (sodium is almost the same as potassium, but with sodium nothing would have happened), the practically identical, the approximate, the or-even, all surrogates, and all patchwork. The differences can be small, but they can lead to radically different consequences, like a railroad's switch points; the chemist's trade consists in good part in being aware of these differences, knowing them close up, and foreseeing their effects. And not only the chemist's trade.

NICKEL

I had in a drawer an illuminated parchment on which was written in elegant characters that on Primo Levi, of the Jewish race, had been conferred a degree in Chemistry summa cum laude. It was therefore a dubious document, half glory and half derision, half absolution and half condemnation. It had remained in that drawer since July 1941, and now we were at the end of November. The world was racing to catastrophe, and around me nothing was happening. The Germans had spread like a flood in Poland, Norway, Holland, France, and Yugoslavia and had penetrated the Russian steppes like a knife cutting through butter. The United States did not move to help the English, who remained alone. I could not find work and was wearing myself out looking for any sort of paid occupation; in the next room my father, prostrated by a tumor, was living his last months.

The doorbell rang—it was a tall, thin young man wearing the uniform of the Italian army, and I immediately recognized in him the figure of the messenger, the Mercury who guides souls, or, if one wishes, the annunciatory angel. In short, the person for whom everyone waits, whether he knows it or not, and who brings the heavenly message that changes your life for good or ill, you don't know which until he opens his mouth.

He opened his mouth, and he had a strong Tuscan accent and asked for Dr. Levi, who incredibly was myself (I still wasn't accustomed to the title), introduced himself urbanely, and offered me a job. Who had sent him to me? Another Mercury, Caselli, the inflexible custodian of another man's fame: that "laude" on my diploma had actually served for something.

That I was a Jew the lieutenant apparently knew (in any event, my last name left little room for doubt), but it didn't seem to matter to him. Moreover, it seemed that the business somehow suited him, that he took a bitter and subtle pleasure in breaking the laws of racial separation—in short, he was secretly an ally and sought an ally in me.

The work he offered me was mysterious and quite fascinating. "In some place" there was a mine, from which was taken 2 percent of some useful material (he didn't tell me what) and 98 percent of sterile material, which was piled up in a nearby valley. In this sterile material there was nickel; very little, but its price was so high that its recovery should be given some thought. He had an idea, in fact a cluster of ideas, but he was in the military service and had little free time. I was supposed to replace him, test his ideas in the lab, and then, if possible, together with him, realize them industrially. It was clear that this required my transfer to that "some place," which was then sketchily described. The transfer would take place under a double seal of secrecy. In the first place, for my protection, nobody should know my name nor my abominable origin, because the "some place" was under the control of the military

authorities; and in the second place, to protect his idea, I would have to swear on my honor not to mention it to anyone. Besides, it was clear that one secret would reinforce the other and that therefore, to a certain degree, my condition as an outcast couldn't have been more opportune.

What was his idea, and where was this "some place"? The lieutenant bowed out there; until my final acceptance he could not tell me much, that was obvious. In any case, the idea consisted in an attack on the sterile material in a gaseous phase, and the "some place" was a few hours' journey from Turin. I quickly consulted with my parents. They agreed: with my father's illness the house had an urgent need of money. As for me, I had not the slightest doubt: I felt sapped by my inactivity, certain of my chemistry, and eager to put it to the test. Besides, the lieutenant had aroused my curiosity and I liked him.

One could see that he wore the uniform with revulsion; his choice of me must not have been dictated solely by practical considerations. He talked about Fascism and the war with reticence and a sinister gaiety that I had no trouble interpreting. It was the ironic gaiety of a whole generation of Italians, intelligent and honest enough to reject Fascism, too skeptical to oppose it actively, too young to passively accept the tragedy that was taking shape and to despair of the future; a generation to which I myself would have belonged if the providential racial laws had not intervened to bring me to a precocious maturity and guide me in my choice.

The lieutenant acknowledged my consent and without wasting time gave me an appointment at the railroad station for the next day. Preparations? I didn't need very much: certainly no documents (I would begin work incognito, without a name or with a false name—we'd see about that later on); a few heavy suits (my climbing outfits would go very well), a shirt, books if I wished. As for the rest, no problem: I would find a heated room, a lab, regular meals with a family of workers, and my colleagues were good people with whom, however, he advised me not to become too intimate for obvious reasons.

We left, got off the train, and reached the mine after a climb 63 of five kilometers surrounded by a forest sparkling with hoar-frost. The lieutenant, who was briskly businesslike, introduced me summarily to the director, a young, tall, vigorous engineer who was even more businesslike and who evidently had already been told about me. I was taken into the lab, where a singular creature awaited me: a rather raw-boned girl of eighteen, with fiery red hair and green, slanting, mischievous, alert eyes. I learned that she would be my assistant.

During the meal which, exceptionally, was offered to me on the office's premises, the radio broadcast the news of the Japanese attack on Pearl Harbor and Japan's declaration of war on the United States. My fellow diners (a number of clerks, besides the lieutenant) greeted the announcement in various ways: some, and among these the lieutenant himself, with reserve and cautious glances at me; others, with worried comments; still others, belligerently insisting on the by now proven invincibility of the Japanese and German armies.

So the "some place" had become localized in space, without, however, losing any of its magic. Yes, all mines are magical per se, and always have been. The entrails of the earth swarm with gnomes, kobolds (cobalt!), *nickel*, German "little demon" or "sprite," and from which we derive the word nickel, creatures who can be generous and let you find a treasure beneath the tip of your pickax, or deceive and bedazzle you, making modest pyrites glitter like gold, or disguising zinc in the garb of tin: and in fact, many are the minerals whose names have roots that signify "deception, fraud, bedazzlement."

This mine too had its magic, its wild enchantment. On a squat, bleak hill, all jagged rocks and stumps, was sunk a cyclopean, cone-shaped gorge, an artificial crater, four hundred meters in diameter: it was in every way similar to the schematic representations of Hell in the synoptic tables of Dante's *Divine Comedy*. Along the encircling tiers, day by day, were exploded dynamite charges: the slope of the cone's walls was graded at the indispensable minimum so that the material shaken loose would roll down to the bottom but without gaining too much speed. At the bottom, in Lucifer's place, stood a ponderous rolling shutter; beneath this was a shallow vertical pit which led into a long horizontal tunnel; this in turn debouched in the open air on the side of the hill, just above the mine's main building. In the tunnel an armored train shuttled back and forth: a small but powerful locomotive positioned the cars one by one under the shutter so that they could be filled, then dragged them out to look again at the stars.

The plant was built in a tier along the slope of the hill and beneath the tunnel's opening; in it the mineral was shattered in a huge crusher that the director described to me and demonstrated with almost childlike enthusiasm. It was a bell turned upside down, or, if one wished, the corolla of a bindweed, four meters in diameter and constructed of massive steel: at its center, suspended from above and guided from below, swung a gigantic clapper. The oscillation was slight, barely visible, but was enough to split in the blink of an eye the mass of rock which poured down from the train: the rocks were split, pressed together lower down, split again, and came out below in fragments as large as a man's head. The operation proceeded in the midst of an apocalyptic uproar, a cloud of dust which could be seen down on the plain. The material was crushed again until it became gravel, then dried out and sifted; and it wasn't difficult to figure out that the final purpose of that gigantic labor was to extract a miserable 2 percent of asbestos which was trapped in those rocks. All the rest, thousands of tons a day, was dumped at random into the valley.

Year after year, the valley was being filled by a slow avalanche of dust and gravel. The asbestos that still was in it made the mass of material slightly slippery, sluggishly sticky, like a glacier: the enormous gray tongue, dotted with blackish rocks, crept laboriously, ponderously downhill, about ten meters a year; it exerted so much pressure on the walls of the valley as to produce deep transverse fissures in the rock; yearly it moved a few inches several of the buildings erected too far down. I lived in one of them, called the "submarine" precisely because of its quiet downward drift.

There was asbestos everywhere, like ashy snow. If you left a book for a few hours on the table and then picked it up, you found its profile in negative; the roofs were covered by a thick layer of dust, which on rainy days soaked through like a sponge, and then suddenly would slide and crash violently to the ground. The head foreman in the mine, called Antaeus, was an obese giant with a thick black beard who actually seemed to draw his strength from Mother Earth. He told me that, years before, a persistent rain had washed many tons of asbestos from the walls of the mine; the asbestos had accumulated at the bottom of the cone over the open valve, secretly setting like a plug. Nobody had attached much importance to the matter, but it had continued to rain, the cone acted as a funnel, a lake of twenty thousand cubic meters of water had formed over the plug, and still nobody had given the matter any thought. He, Antaeus, saw trouble coming and had insisted that the then director do something about it: being the good mine foreman that he was he favored a nice big dynamite charge exploded without ado on the bottom of the lake; but what with this and that, it might be dangerous, you could damage the valve, best to get the advice of the administrative council, nobody wanted to decide, and meanwhile the mine, with its malign genius, decided by itself.

While the wise men were deliberating, a dull roar was heard, the plug had given way, the water sank in the pit and tunnel, swept away the train with all its cars, and laid waste the plant. Antaeus showed me the marks left by the flood, a good two meters above the inclined plane.

The workers and miners (who in the local jargon were called "minors") came from the neighboring villages, walking perhaps two hours over the mountain paths. The clerks lived on the spot. The plain was only five kilometers away, but for all purposes the mine was a small autonomous republic. At that time of rationing and black market there were no supply problems up there; nobody knew how this was, but everyone had everything. Many clerks had their own truck gardens, around the square villa that housed the offices; some of them even had chicken coops. Several times one clerk's chickens would invade the truck garden of another, damaging it, and this produced tiresome disputes and feuds, which were ill-suited to the serenity of the place and the director's curt, no-nonsense nature. He had cut through the tangle in a manner worthy of him: he had ordered a Flobert shotgun and hung it on a nail in his office. Anyone who from the window saw a foreign chicken scratching around in his truck garden had the right to take the shotgun and shoot it twice: but the chicken had to be caught in the act. If the chicken died on the field, the corpse belonged to the shooter; this was the law. During the first days after the ruling, there had been many dashes for the gun and shootings, while all those not involved bet on the outcome, but then the trespassing stopped.

Other marvelous stories were told to me, like the story about Signor Pistamiglio's dog. This Signor Pistamiglio, when I got there, had been gone for years, but his memory was still alive and, as often happens, had acquired a gilded patina of legend. So then this Signor Pistamiglio was an excellent section chief, no longer young, a bachelor, full of common sense, esteemed by all, and his dog was a very beautiful German shepherd, equally upright and esteemed.

There came a certain Christmas and four of the fattest turkeys in the town down in the valley disappeared. Too bad: thieves had been suspected, a fox, and that was the end of it. But another winter came and this time seven turkeys disappeared between November and December. The thefts were reported to the local carabinieri, but nobody would have ever solved the mystery if Signor Pistamiglio himself had not let slip one word too many one evening when he'd drunk a bit. The turkey thieves were the two of them, he and his dog. On Sunday he took his dog to the town, roamed about among the farms,   67 and showed him which were the most beautiful and least guarded turkeys; case by case he explained to him the best strategy; then they came back to the mine and at night he would set him free, and the dog arrived invisibly, slithering along the walls like a real wolf, jumped over the fence around the chicken coop or dug a passage under it, killed the turkey silently, and brought it back to his accomplice. It does not appear that Signor Pistamiglio sold the turkeys; according to the most accredited version, he gave them as gifts to his lovers, who were numerous, old, ugly, and scattered throughout the foothills of the Piedmontese Alps.

But many, many stories were told; from what could be gathered, all fifty of the mine's inhabitants had reacted on each other, two by two, as in combinatorial analysis, that is to say, everyone with all the others, and especially every man with all the women, old maids or married, and every woman with all the men. All I had to do was select two names at random, better if of different sex, and ask a third person: "What happened with those two?" and lo and behold, a splendid story was unfolded for me, since everyone knew the story of everyone else. It is not clear why these events, often quite complicated and always intimate, were told so offhandedly, particularly to me of all people, who on the contrary could tell nothing to anyone, not even my real name. But it appears that this is my fate (and I'm definitely not complaining about it): I am one of those people to whom many things are told.

I recorded in various versions a remote saga going back to a period much before Signor Pistamiglio's. There had been a time when, in the mine's offices, they had had a real Gomorrah. During that legendary season, every evening, when the five-thirty siren sounded, none of the clerks went home. At that signal, liquor and mattresses suddenly popped up from among the desks, and an orgy erupted that embraced everything and everyone, young pubescent stenographers and balding accoun-

tants, starting with the then director all the way down to the disabled doormen: the sad round of mining paperwork gave way suddenly, every evening, to a boundless interclass fornication, public and variously intertwined. No survivors had lived down to our day to provide direct testimony: a series of disastrous balance sheets had forced the board of governors in Milan to carry out a drastic, purifying intervention. Nobody except for Signora Bortolasso, who, I was assured, knew everything, had seen everything, but was not talking because of her extreme shyness.

Signora Bortolasso, in any case, never talked with anyone, outside the strict necessities of work. Before she had her present name she was called Gina delle Benne: at nineteen, already a typist in the office, she had fallen in love with a young, slim, red-headed miner who, without really reciprocating, showed himself nevertheless ready to accept her love; but her "folks" had been adamant. They had spent money on her studies and she had to show her gratitude by making a good marriage and not hooking up with just anybody; and what's more, since the girl refused to be reasonable, they would see to it: either drop that redhead or get out of the house and the mine.

Gina was willing to wait until her twenty-first birthday (which was only two years away): but the redhead didn't wait for her. He showed up one Sunday with another woman, then with a third, and wound up marrying a fourth. Gina then made a cruel decision: if she couldn't bind herself to the man she cared for, the only one, well then, there would not be any other. Not a nun; she had modern ideas: but she forbade herself marriage forever in a refined and merciless manner, that is, by getting married. She was by now almost an executive, needed by the management, endowed with an iron memory and proverbial diligence: and she let everyone know, her parents and her bosses, that she intended to marry Bortolasso, the mine's simpleton.

This Bortolasso was a middle-aged laborer, strong as a mule and dirty as a pig. He most likely was not a real simpleton: it is more probable that he belonged to that species of human being of whom one says in Piedmont that they play the fool so as not to pay for the salt: sheltering behind the immunity granted the weak-minded, Bortolasso performed with extreme negligence the job of gardener—with a negligence that verged on rudimentary cunning. Very well, the world had declared him irresponsible and now it had to tolerate him as such, indeed give him a living and take care of him.

Asbestos drenched by rain is hard to extract, so the rain gauge at the mine was very important. It was placed in the middle of a flowerbed, and the director himself took the readings. Bortolasso, who every morning watered the flowerbed, got the habit of also watering the rain gauge, severely falsifying the data for the costs of extraction. The director (not immediately) realized this and gave him orders to stop. "So then he likes it dry," Bortolasso reasoned; and after every rain he would go and open the valve under the instrument.

When I arrived at the mine the situation had been stabilized for some time. Gina, now Signora Bortolasso, was about thirty-five: the modest beauty of her face had grown stiff and fixed in a tense, alert mask and bore the manifest stigma of a protracted virginity. For a virgin she had remained, they all knew it because Bortolasso told it to everyone. This had been the agreement at the time of the marriage; he had accepted it, even if later, almost every night, he tried to violate the woman's bed. But she had defended herself furiously and still defended herself—never, never would a man, and most of all that one, be permitted to touch her.

These nightly battles of the sad couple had become the talk of the mine, and one of its few attractions. On one of the first mild evenings, a group of aficionados invited me to come along with them to hear what happened. I refused and they returned disappointed soon after: they had heard only a trombone playing "Faccetta Nera."* They explained to me that sometimes this

*"Little Black Face," a Fascist song popularized at the time that Italy invaded Ethiopia, in 1936—TRANS.

happened: he was a musical simpleton and would blow off steam in that way.

I fell in love with my work from the very first day, although it entailed nothing more at that stage than quantitative analysis of rock samples: attack with hydrofluoric acid, down comes iron with ammonia, down comes nickel (how little! a pinch of red sediment) with dimethylglyoxime, down comes magnesium with phosphate, always the same, every blessed day—in itself, it was not very stimulating. But stimulating and new was another sensation: the sample to be analyzed was no longer an anonymous, manufactured powder, a materialized quiz: it was a piece of rock, the earth's entrail, torn from the earth by the explosive's force; and on the basis of the daily data of the analysis little by little was born a map, the portrait of the subterranean veins. For the first time after seventeen years of schoolwork, of Greek verbs and the history of the Peloponnesian War, the things I had learned were beginning to be useful to me. Quantitative analysis, so devoid of emotion, heavy as granite, came alive, true, useful, when part of serious and concrete work. It was useful: it was part of a plan, a tessera in a mosaic. The analytical method I followed was no longer a bookish dogma, it was put to the test every day, it could be refined, made to conform with our aims, by a subtle play of reason, of trial and error. To make a mistake was no longer a vaguely comic accident that spoils an exam for you or affects your marks: to make a mistake was similar to when you go climbing—a contest, an act of attention, a step up that makes you more worthy and fit.

The girl in the lab was called Alida. She watched my neophyte's enthusiasms without sharing them; she was in fact surprised and somewhat annoyed. Her presence was not unpleasant. She was a *liceo* graduate, quoted Pindar and Sappho, the daughter of a completely innocuous small local Fascist official, was cunning and slothful, and didn't give a damn about anything, least of all the analysis of rock, which she had learned to perform mechanically from the lieutenant. She too, like all the people up there, had interacted with several persons and did not make a mystery of it with me, thanks to that curious gift for garnering confessions which I mentioned before. She had fought with many women because of vague rivalries, had fallen in love a little with many men, a great deal with one, and was engaged to still another, a gray, unpretentious fellow, an employee in the Technical Office who came from her town and whom her family had picked for her. About this, too, she didn't give a damn. What could she do about it? Rebel? Leave? No, she was a girl from a good family, her future was children and the kitchen stove, Sappho and Pindar were things of the past and nickel an abstruse stopgap. She worked listlessly in the lab while waiting for that so little longed-for marriage, negligently washing the precipitates, weighing the nickel dimethylglyoxime, and I had hard work convincing her that it was not quite the thing to pad the results of the analyses: something she tended to do, in fact she confessed to having done often, since, she said, it didn't cost anybody anything, and pleased the director, the lieutenant, and myself.

What, after all, was that chemistry over which the lieutenant and I racked our brains? Water and fire, nothing else, like in the kitchen. A less appetizing kitchen, that's all: with penetrating or disgusting smells instead of the domestic kind; for the rest, there too aprons, mixing, burned hands, and washing up at the end of the day. No escape for Alida. She listened with devout compunction and at the same time Italian skepticism to my tales of life in Turin: these were heavily censored because in fact both she and I had to play the game of my anonymity. Nevertheless something did emerge: if nothing else, from my reticences themselves. After some weeks I realized that I was no longer a nameless person: I was a certain Doctor Levi who must not be called Levi, neither in the second nor the third person, due to good manners, and in order to avoid a mess. In the mine's gossipy and easygoing atmosphere, a disparity between my indeterminate state as an outcast and my visible mildness of manner leaped to the eye, and——Alida admitted this to me—— was lengthily discussed and variously interpreted: I was everything from an agent of the OVRA, the Fascist secret police, to someone with high-class connections.

Going down into the valley was uncomfortable, and for me not very prudent; since I could not visit anyone, my evenings at the mine were interminable. Sometimes I stayed in the lab past quitting time or went back there after dinner to study, or to meditate on the problem of nickel. At other times I shut myself in to read Mann's Joseph stories in my monastic cell in the submarine. On nights when the moon was up I often took long solitary walks through the wild countryside around the mine, all the way up to the brim of the crater, or halfway up on the back of the gray, craggy dump chute, shaken by mysterious creaks and shivers as if some busy gnomes really nested there: the darkness was punctuated by the distant howls of dogs in the invisible valley bottom.

These roamings granted me a truce from the grim awareness of my father dying in Turin, of the American defeats at Bataan, the German victories in the Crimea, in short, of the open trap which was about to spring shut: it gave birth in me to a new bond, more sincere than the rhetoric about nature learned at school, with those brambles and stones which were my island and my freedom, a freedom I would perhaps soon lose.

For that rock without peace I felt a fragile and precarious affection: with it I had contracted a double bond, first in the exploits with Sandro, then here, trying as a chemist to wrest away its treasure. From this rocky love and these asbestos-filled solitudes, on some other of those long nights were born two stories of islands and freedom, the first I felt inclined to write after the torments of compositions in *liceo*: one story fantasized about a remote precursor of mine, a hunter of lead instead of nickel; the other, ambiguous and mercurial, I had taken from a reference to the island of Tristan da Cunha that I happened to see during that period.

73

The lieutenant, who was doing his military service in Turin, came up to the mine only one day a week. He would check my work and give me instructions and advice for the coming week, and proved to be an excellent chemist and a tenacious and acute researcher. After a short period of orientation, alongside the routine of daily analyses, a project with much higher aims began to take shape.

In the mine's rock there was indeed nickel, but very little: from our analyses it showed an average content of 0.2 percent. Ridiculous, in comparison to the minerals mined by my antipodal colleague-rivals in Canada and New Caledonia. But perhaps the raw material could be enriched? Under the lieutenant's guidance I tried all possible methods: by magnetic separation, by flotation, by levigation, by sifting, with heavy liquids, with the shaking plate. I did not get anywhere: nothing concentrated; in all the fractions the percentage of nickel remained obstinately the same as the first. Nature was not helping us: we concluded that the nickel accompanying the bivalent iron took its place vicariously, followed it like an evanescent shadow, a minuscule brother: 0.2 percent of nickel, 8 percent of iron. All the reagents imaginable for nickel should have been employed in doses forty times greater, even without taking into account the magnesium. An economically desperate enterprise. At moments of weariness I perceived the rock that encircled me, the green serpentine of the Alpine foothills, in all its sidereal, hostile, extraneous hardness: in comparison, the trees of the valley, by now already dressed for spring, were like us, also people who do not speak but feel the heat and the frost, enjoy and suffer, are born and die, fling out pollen with the wind, obscurely follow the sun in its travels. Not the rock: it does not house any energy, it is extinguished since primordial times, pure hostile passivity; a massive fortress that I had to pull down bastion by bastion to get my hands on the hidden sprite, the capricious *kupfernickel* which jumps out now here, now there, elusive and malign, with long perked ears, always ready to flee from the blows of the investigating pickax, leaving you with nothing to show for it.

74

But this is no longer the time for sprites, *nickel*, and kobolds. We are chemists, that is, hunters: ours are "the two experiences of adult life" of which Pavese spoke, success and failure, to kill the white whale or wreck the ship; one should not surrender to incomprehensible matter, one must not just sit down. We are here for this—to make mistakes and to correct ourselves, to stand the blows and hand them out. We must never feel disarmed: nature is immense and complex, but it is not impermeable to the intelligence; we must circle around it, pierce and probe it, look for the opening or make it. My weekly conversations with the lieutenant sounded like war plans.

Among the many attempts we had made there also was that of reducing the rock with hydrogen. We had placed the mineral, finely ground, in a porcelain boat; had placed this in turn in a quartz tube; and through the tube, heated from the outside, we had pushed a current of hydrogen in the hope that this would strip the oxygen bound to the nickel and leave it reduced, that is, naked, in its metallic state. Metallic nickel, like iron, is magnetic, and therefore, according to this hypothesis, it would have been easy to separate it from the rest, alone or with the iron, simply by means of a small magnet. But, after the treatment, we had vainly agitated a powerful magnet in the watery suspension of our powder: we had only gotten a trace of iron. Clear and sad: hydrogen, under these conditions, did not reduce anything; the nickel, together with the iron, must be firmly lodged in the serpentine's structure, combined with the silicate and water, satisfied (so to speak) with its state and averse to assuming another.

But say one tried to pull that structure apart. The idea came to me as one switches on a light, one day when by chance there fell into my hands an old dusty diagram, the work of some unknown predecessor of mine; it showed the loss of weight in the mine's asbestos as a function of temperature. The asbestos lost a little water at 150° centigrade, then remained apparently unaltered until about 800° centigrade; here one noted an abrupt step down with a fall in weight of 12 percent, and the author had remarked: "becomes fragile." Now serpentine is the father of asbestos: if asbestos decomposes at 800° centigrade, serpentine should do so also; and, since a chemist does not think, indeed does not live, without models, I idly went about representing them for myself, drawing on paper long chains of silicon, oxygen, iron, and magnesium, with a little nickel caught between their links, and then the same chains after the smash reduced to short stubs, with the nickel flushed out of its den and exposed to attack; and I did not feel much different from the remote hunter of Altamira who painted an antelope on the rock wall so that the next day's hunt would be lucky.

The propitiatory ceremonies did not last long: the lieutenant was not there, but he could arrive from one hour to the next, and I was afraid that he would not accept, or would not readily accept, my very unorthodox hypothesis of work. But I felt it itch all over my skin: what's done is done, best get to work immediately.

There is nothing more vivifying than a hypothesis. Watched with an amused and skeptical expression by Alida, who, since it was now late in the afternoon, kept looking ostentatiously at her wristwatch, I set to work like a whirlwind. In a moment the apparatus was mounted, the thermostat set at 800° centigrade, the pressure regulator on the tank set, the fluxmeter put in order. I heated the material for half an hour, then reduced the temperature and passed the hydrogen through for another hour: by now it was dark, the girl had gone, all was silence against the backdrop of the grim hum of the Grading Department, which also worked at night. I felt part conspirator, part alchemist.

When the time came, I took the porcelain boat out of the quartz tube, let it cool off in the vacuum, then dispersed in water the powder, which had turned from greenish to a dirty yellow: a thing which seemed to me a good sign. I picked up the magnet and set to work. Each time I took the magnet out of the water, it brought with it a tuft of brown powder: I removed it delicately with filter paper and put it aside, perhaps a milligram each time; for the analysis to be well-founded at least a half gram of material was needed, that is, several hours of work. I decided to stop about midnight: to interrupt the separation, I mean to say, because at no cost would I have put off the beginning of the analysis. For this, since it involved a magnetic fraction (and therefore presumably poor in silicates), and yielding to my haste, I there and then tried a simplified variant. At three in the morning I had the result: no longer the usual pink little cloud of nickel-dimethylglyoxime but rather a visibly abundant precipitate. Filtered, washed, dried, and weighed. The final datum appeared to me written in letters of fire on the slide rule: 6 percent of nickel, the rest iron. A victory: even without a further separation, an alloy to be sent to the electric oven as is. I returned to the submarine when it was almost dawn with an acute desire to go immediately and wake the director, telephone the lieutenant, and roll around on the dark fields, which were dripping wet with dew. I was thinking many foolish things, and I was not thinking of anything sensible and sad.

I was thinking of having opened a door with a key, and of possessing the key to many doors, perhaps to all of them. I was thinking of having thought of something that nobody else had yet thought, not even in Canada or New Caledonia, and I felt invincible and untouchable even when faced by close enemies, closer each month. Finally, I was thinking of having had a far from ignoble revenge on those who had declared me biologically inferior.

I was not thinking that if the method of extraction I had caught sight of could have found industrial application, the nickel produced would have entirely ended up in Fascist Italy's and Hitler Germany's armor plate and artillery shells. I was not thinking that during those very months there had been discovered in Albania deposits of nickel mineral before which ours could go and hide, and along with it every project of mine, the director's, and the lieutenant's. I did not foresee that my interpretation of the magnetic separability of nickel was substantially mistaken, as the lieutenant showed me a few days later, as soon as I told him of my results. Nor did I foresee that the director, after having shared my enthusiasm for a few days, threw a wet blanket on mine and his when he realized that there did not exist in commerce any magnetic selector capable of separating a material in the form of a fine powder, and that on cruder powders my method could not function.

And yet this story does not end here. Despite the many years that have passed, the liberalization of exchanges, and the fall in the international price of nickel, the news of the enormous wealth that lies in that valley in the form of rubble accessible to everyone still sets fire to the imagination. Not far from the mine, in cellars, stables, on the borderline between chemistry and white magic, there are still people who go at night to the rubble heaps and come back with bags of gray gravel, grind it, cook it, treat it with ever new reagents. The fascination of buried wealth, of two kilos of a noble silvery metal bound to a thousand kilos of sterile stone which is thrown away, has not yet died out.

Nor have the two mineral tales which I wrote then disappeared. They have had a troubled fate, almost as troubled as my own: they have suffered bombings and escapes, I had given them up for lost, and I found them recently while going through papers forgotten for decades. I did not want to abandon them: the reader will find them here in the succeeding pages, inserted, like a prisoner's dream of escape, between these tales of militant chemistry.

LEAD

*My name is Rodmund and I come from far away. My country is
called Thiuda; at least we call it that, but our neighbors, that
is, our enemies, use different names for us—Saksa, Nemet,
Alaman. My country is different from this one; it has great
forests and rivers, long winters, swamps, mists and rain. My
people—I mean those who speak my language—are shepherds, hunters, and warriors: they do not like to cultivate the
land, indeed they scorn those who do cultivate it, drive their
flocks on their fields, sack their villages, and make slaves of
their women. I am neither a shepherd nor a warrior; I am not
even a hunter, although my trade is not very different from a*   79

hunter's. It ties me to the land, but I am free: I am not a peasant.

My father and all of us Rodmunds in the paternal line have always plied this trade, which consists in knowing a certain heavy rock, finding it in distant countries, heating it in a certain way that we know, and extracting black lead from it. Near my village there was a large bed; it is said that it had been discovered by one of my ancestors whom they called Rodmund Blue Teeth. It is a village of lead-smiths; everyone there knows how to smelt and work it, but only we Rodmunds know how to find the rock and make sure it is the real lead rock, and not one of the many heavy rocks that the gods have strewn over the mountain so as to deceive man. It is the gods who make the veins of metals grow under the ground, but they keep them secret, hidden; he who finds them is almost their equal, and so the gods do not love him and try to bewilder him. They do not love us Rodmunds: but we don't care.

Now, in five or six generations the bed has been exhausted: someone has suggested following it below the ground, digging tunnels, and even tried to do it and lost by it; finally the opinion of the more prudent prevailed. All the men have resumed their former trades, but not I: just as the lead, without us, does not see the light, so we cannot live without lead. Ours is an art that makes us rich, but it also makes us die young. Some say that this happens because the metal enters our blood and slowly impoverishes it; others think instead that it is a revenge of the gods, but in any case it matters little to us Rodmunds that our lives are short, because we are rich, respected, and see the world. In fact the case of my ancestor with the blue teeth is exceptional, because the deposit he had discovered was exceptionally rich: in general, we prospectors are also travelers. He himself, they told me, came from far away, from a country where the sun is cold and never sets, the people live in houses made of ice, and in the sea swim monsters a thousand strides long.

So, after six generations in one place, I began traveling again, in search of rock to smelt or to be smelted by other people; teaching them the art in exchange for gold. We Rodmunds are wizards, that's what we are: we change lead into gold.

I left by myself, heading southward, when I was still young. I traveled for four years, from region to region, avoiding the plains, climbing up the mountain valleys, tapping with my hammer, finding little or nothing: in the summer I worked in the fields; in the winter I wove baskets or spent the gold I had brought with me. By myself, I have said: for us, women serve to provide a male child, so that the race does not die out, but we don't take them along. What use would they serve? They don't learn how to find the rock, and in fact, if they touch it when they have their period it crumbles into dead sand and ashes. Better the girls you meet along the way, good for a night or a month, with whom you can make merry without thinking of tomorrow, as instead wives do. It is better to live our tomorrows alone: when the flesh begins to become loose and pale, the belly pains, hair and teeth fall out, gums turn gray, then it is better to be alone.

I arrived at a place from which, on clear days, you could see a chain of mountains to the south. In the spring I began walking again, determined to reach them: I was completely fed up with that sticky, soft earth, good for nothing, good for making clay ocarinas, lacking both secrets and virtue. In the mountains it is different: the rocks, which are the bones of the 81 earth, can be seen uncovered, they ring out under your hobnailed boots, and it is easy to distinguish the different qualities: the plain is not for us. I would ask around where the easiest mountain pass was. I also asked if they had lead, where they bought it, and how much they paid for it: the more money they paid, the more I searched in the vicinity. Sometimes they didn't even know what lead was; when I showed them the chunk of it that I always carry in my bag they laughed at feeling it so soft, and derisively asked me if in my country lead is also used to make ploughs and swords. Most times, however, I could not understand them or make them understand me: bread, milk, a cot, a girl, the direction to take the next day, and that's all.

I got through a broad pass at the height of the summer, with a sun that at midday was almost perpendicular over my head, and yet there were still splotches of snow on the upland meadows. Just a bit lower down were flocks, shepherds, and paths: you could see the bottom of the valley, so deep that it still seemed immersed in the night. I descended, found villages, one rather large village on a stream, where the mountain folk came down to barter livestock, horses, cheese, pelts, and a red liquid they called wine. I almost burst out laughing whenever I heard them speak: their language was a crude and indistinct gurgle, an animal-like gur-gur, so much so that it was surprising to see that they nevertheless actually had weapons and tools like ours, some of them even more ingenious and elaborate. The women spun, as they did back home. They build houses of rock, not so pretty but solid; some houses, though, were made of wood, suspended a few feet above the ground

since they rested on four or six wooden blocks topped by disks of smooth stone; I believe these stones served to prevent the invasion of mice, and this seemed to me an intelligent invention. The roofs were not made of straw but of broad, flat stones. They did not know beer.

I immediately saw that on high, along the valley's sides, there were holes in the rock and cascades of rubble: the sign that in these parts too some people were prospecting. But I did not ask any questions to avoid arousing suspicion; a foreigner like myself aroused too much already. I went down to the stream, which was rather swift (I remember that its water was turbid and a dingy white, as if it had been mixed with milk, something which in my parts was unheard of), and I set about patiently examining the stones: this is one of our tricks, the stones in a stream come from afar and speak clearly to him who understands. There was a little of everything: flint stones, green stones, lime stones, granite, iron-bearing stones, even a little of what we call galmeida, all stuff that did not interest me; and yet I had the fixed idea that in a valley formed like that, with certain white striations on the red rock and with so much iron thereabouts, lead rocks could not be missing.

I walked down along the stream, partly on the boulders, partly wading wherever I could, like a hunting dog, with my eyes glued to the ground, when lo and behold! a little below the confluence with another, smaller stream, I saw a stone among millions of other stones, a stone almost the same as all the others, a dingy white stone with small black speckles, which brought me to a halt, tense and motionless, exactly like a hunting dog pointing. I picked it up. It was heavy. Next to it was another like it but smaller. We rarely make mistakes: but just to be sure I crushed it and took a fragment as big as a nut   83 *along with me to test it. A good prospector, a serious one, who does not want to tell lies either to others or himself, should not trust in appearances, because the rock, which seems dead, instead is full of deception: sometimes it changes its nature even while you're digging, like certain snakes that change color so you won't see them. A good prospector, therefore, carries everything with him: a clay crucible, pieces of charcoal, touchwood and steel, and another instrument that is secret and I can't mention and is used precisely to find out whether the rock is good or not.*

That evening I found an out-of-the-way spot, built a hearth, on which I put the well-layered crucible, heated it for half an hour, and then let it cool. I broke it open and there it was—the shiny heavy little disk which can be scored by your fingernail, which makes your heart leap with joy and the fatigue of the long walk vanish from your legs, and which we call "the little king."

At this point we are far from finished; on the contrary, most of the work is still to be done. You have to go back up the stream, and at every branching look around to see whether the good stone continues to right or left. I went up for quite a distance along the big stream and the stone was always there but became more and more sparse; then the valley narrowed to a gorge so profound and steep that climbing it was out of the question. I asked the shepherds thereabouts and they gave me to understand by dint of gestures and grunts that there really was no way of getting around that gorge, but if you went back down to the big valley you would find a small road, about so wide, which ran through a pass they called something like Tringo and descended just above the gorge, ending up in a

place where there were horned beasts that mooed and therefore

(I thought) also grazing land, shepherds, bread, and milk. I started walking, easily found the road and Tringo, and from there went down to a very beautiful country.

Straight in front of me in a long tunnel-like view I saw a valley green with larches, and in the distance mountains white with snow at the height of the summer: the valley ended at my feet in a vast meadow dotted with huts and flocks. I was tired; I walked farther down and stopped by the shepherds. They were distrustful, but they knew (even too well) the value of gold, and they put me up for a few days without bothering me. I took advantage of this to learn a few words of their language— they called mountains "pen," meadows "tza," the snow of summer "roisa," sheep "fea," their houses "bait," which are made of rock in the lower part, where they keep the livestock, and of wood above, with stone rests as I have already said, where they live and store hay and provisions. They were cantankerous people, who spoke little, but they had no weapons and did not treat me badly.

When I was rested I resumed my search, still with the stream system, and I wound up slipping into a valley parallel to the larch valley, long, narrow, and deserted, without meadows or woods. The stream which ran through it was rich in good rock: I felt I was close to what I was searching for. It took me three days, sleeping in the open: in fact, without sleeping at all, I was that impatient, passing the night staring at the sky so that dawn would break soon.

The deposit was quite out of the way, in a very steep gully: the white rock cropped out here and there amid sickly grass, within a hand's reach, and all you had to do was dig two or three feet to find the black rock, the richest of all, which I had never yet seen but which my father had described to me. A 85 compact rock without slag, to put a hundred men to work for a hundred years. What was strange was that someone must have already been there: you could see, half hidden behind a rock (which certainly had been put there on purpose), the opening to a tunnel, which must have been very old, because from its vault hung stalactites as long as my fingers. On the ground there were stakes of rotted wood and a few corroded bone fragments; the rest must have been carried off by the foxes—in fact there were footprints of foxes and perhaps of wolves: but a half skull that protruded from the mud was certainly human. This is a difficult thing to explain, but it has already happened more than once that someone, who knows when, coming from who knows where, at some remote time, perhaps before the Flood, finds a vein, does not say anything to anyone, tries by himself to dig out the rock, leaves his bones there, and then the centuries pass. My father told me that in whatever tunnel or cave you may dig you find the bones of the dead.

In short, the deposit was there: I made my tests, I built as best I could a furnace there in the open, I went down and came back up with wood, I melted down as much lead as I could carry on my back, and I returned to the valley. I didn't say anything to the people on the pastureland; I continued down the Tringo and came to the large village on the other side, which was called Sales. It was market day, and I put myself on show with my piece of lead in my hand. A few people began to stop, to weigh it and ask me questions, of which I only understood half; it was clear that they wanted to know what it was good for, how much it cost, and where it came from. Then an alert-looking fellow with a plaited woolen cap came up to me, and we understood each other pretty well. I showed him that you could beat that stuff with a hammer: in fact, right *there and then I found a hammer and a curbstone and showed him how easy it is to fashion it into slabs and sheets: then I explained to him that with the sheets, welding them on one side with a red-hot iron, you could make pipes. I told him that wooden pipes, for example, the rainpipes in that town Sales, leak and rot; I explained to him that bronze pipes are hard to make and when they are used for drinking water cause stomach trouble, and that instead lead pipes last forever and can be joined together very easily. Putting on a solemn face, I also took a random shot and explained to him that with a sheet of lead you can also line coffins for the dead, so that they don't grow worms but become dry and thin, and so the soul too is not dispersed, which is a fine advantage; and still with lead you can cast small funeral statues, not shiny like bronze, but in fact a bit dark, a bit subdued, as is suitable to objects of mourning. Since I saw that these matters interested him greatly, I explained that, if one goes beyond appearances, lead is actually the metal of death: because it brings on death, because its weight is a desire to fall, and to fall is a property of corpses, because its very color is dulled-dead, because it is the metal of the planet Tuisto, which is the slowest of the planets, that is, the planet of the dead. I also told him that, in my opinion, lead is a material different from all other materials, a metal which you feel is tired, perhaps tired of transforming itself and that does not want to transform itself anymore: the ashes of who knows how many other elements full of life, which thousands upon thousands of years ago were burned in their own fire. These are things I really think; it is not that I invented them to close the deal. That man, whose name was Borvio, listened to all this with his mouth agape, and then he told me that it really must be as I said, and that that planet is sacred to a god* 87 who in his town was called Saturn and is depicted with a scythe. This was the moment to get down to brass tacks, and while he was still there mulling over my blandishments, I asked him for thirty pounds of gold for handing over the deposit, the technique of smelting the lead, and precise instructions on the principal uses of the metal. He made me a counter offer of bronze coins with a boar imprinted on them, coined God knows where, but I made the motion of spitting on them: gold, and cut the nonsense. Anyway, thirty pounds are too much for someone traveling on foot, everyone knows that, and I knew that Borvio knew it: so we concluded the deal for twenty pounds. He insisted that I accompany him to the deposit, which was only right. When we got back to the valley, he gave me the gold: I checked all twenty ingots, found them genuine and of good weight, and we got beautifully drunk on wine to celebrate.

It was also a farewell drunk. It is not that that country did not please me, but many reasons impelled me to continue my journey. First: I wanted to see the warm countries, where they say olives and lemons grow. Second: I wanted to see the sea, not the stormy sea from which came my ancestor with the blue teeth, but the tepid sea, from which comes salt. Third: there's no point in having gold and carrying it on your back, with the continuous terror that at night or during a drinking bout someone will steal it from you. Fourth, and to sum up: I wanted to spend the gold on a sea voyage, to get to know the sea and sailors, because sailors need lead, even if they do not know it.

So I left: I walked for two months, descending a large sad valley until it opened out on a plain. There were meadows and wheat fields and a sharp smell of burnt brushwood which filled me with nostalgia for my country: autumn, in all the countries of the world, has the same smell of dead leaves, of resting earth, of bundles of burning branches, in short, of things which are ending, and you think "forever." I came across a fortified city—there are none as large back home—at the confluence of two rivers; there was a market fair with slaves, meats, wine; filthy, solid, disheveled girls; a tavern with a good fire—and I spent the winter there: it snowed as it does back home. I left in March, and after a month of walking I found the sea, which was not blue but gray, bellowed like a bison, and hurled itself on the land as though it wanted to devour it: at the thought that it never rested, never had rested since the beginning of the world, my courage failed me. But I still continued down the road to the east, along the beach, because the sea fascinated me and I could not tear myself away from it.

I found another city, and I stopped there, also because my gold was beginning to come to an end. They were fishermen and strange folk, who came by ship from various, very distant countries: they bought and sold; at night they fought over the women and knifed each other in the alleyways. Then I too bought a heavy knife made of bronze in a leather sheath, to carry tied to my waist under my clothes. They knew glass but not mirrors; that is, they only had small mirrors of polished bronze, cheap things, the kind that get scratched immediately and distort the colors. If you have lead it is not difficult to make a glass mirror, but I made a fuss about parting with the secret, I told them that it is an art which only we Rodmunds know, that a goddess named Frigga taught it to us, and other foolishness which they swallowed hook, line, and sinker.

I needed money: I looked around me, found near the port a glazier who seemed rather intelligent, and made a deal with him. 89

From him I learned several things—first of all, that glass can be blown: I liked that system a great deal, and I even had him teach it to me, and one day or another I will also try to blow lead or melted bronze (but they are too liquid, I doubt whether I'll succeed). I, however, taught him that on a still-hot pane of glass you can pour melted lead and obtain mirrors not so large but luminous, without flaws, which last for many years. He in fact was rather adept: he had a secret for making colored glass and fashioned variegated glass panes that were beautiful to look at. I was full of enthusiasm for the collaboration and invented a process of making mirrors also with the rounded caps of blown glass, pouring the lead into it or spreading it on the outside: if you looked into them you see yourself either very large or very small, or even all crooked: these mirrors are not liked by women, but all children insist on getting them. Through the summer and fall we sold mirrors to the merchants, who paid well for them; but meanwhile I was talking with them and tried to gather as much information as I could on a region which many of them knew.

It was astounding to see how those people, who actually spent half their lives on the sea, had such confused notions about the cardinal points and distances; but, in short, on one point they were all agreed: that is, that by sailing south, some said a thousand miles, others said ten times farther than that, you came to a land which the sun had burnt to dust, rich in unusual trees and animals, and inhabited by ferocious men with black skin. But many stated as a certainty that halfway along you encountered a large island called Icnusa, which was the island of metals: they told the strangest stories about this island, which was inhabited by giants, whereas the horses, oxen, even rabbits and chickens were tiny; that the women gave orders and fought the wars, while the *men watched over the livestock and spun the wool; that these* giants were devourers of men, especially foreigners; that it was a land of utter whoredom, where the husbands exchanged wives and even the animals coupled haphazardly, wolves with cats, bears with cows; that the women's period of pregnancy lasted only three days, then the women gave birth and immediately told the infant: "Get moving, bring me the scissors and turn on the light, so I can cut your umbilical cord." Still others said that along its coasts there are fortresses built of rock, big as mountains; that everything on that island is made of rock——the points of the spears, the wheels of the wagons, even the women's combs and sewing needles: also the pots to cook with, and that they actually have stones which burn and they set them alight under these pots; that along their roads, to guard the crossroads, there are petrified monsters frightening to look at. I listened to all these things with a grave face, but within myself I was laughing loud enough to burst, because by now I have roamed the world enough and know that all is just like your hometown: for the rest, I too, when I get back and tell stories about the countries I've been in, amuse myself by inventing weird tales; indeed, here they tell fantastic stories about my country——for example, that our buffalo do not have knees and all you have to do to slaughter them is saw through the trees against which they lean at night to rest: their weight breaks the tree; they fall down and cannot get up again.

As to metals, however, they were all in agreement: many merchants and sea captains had brought loads of raw or finished metal from the island to land, but they were crude folk and from their accounts it was hard to understand what metal they were referring to; also because not all spoke the same language and no one spoke mine, and there was a great confusion of terms. They said, for example, "kalibe" and there was absolutely no way to figure out whether they meant iron, silver, or bronze. Others called "sider" either iron or ice, and they were so ignorant as to insist that the ice in the mountains, with the passing of the centuries and beneath the weight of the rock, hardens and first becomes rock crystal and later iron-bearing rock.

To put it bluntly, I was fed up with these female occupations and wanted to go and see this Icnusa. I handed over to the glazier my share in the business, and with that money, plus the money I had made from the mirrors, I got passage on board a cargo ship; but you don't leave in the winter, there is the north wind, or the west wind, or the south wind, or the southwest wind—in brief, it appears that no wind is good, and that until April the best thing is to stay on land, get drunk, bet your shirt on the dice games, and get some girl in the port pregnant.

We left in April. The ship was loaded with jugs of wine; besides the owner there was the crew chief, four sailors, and twenty rowers chained to their benches. The crew chief came from Kriti and was a big liar: he told stories about a country where there lived men called Big Ears, who have ears so huge that they wrap themselves in them to sleep in the winter, and about animals called Alfil with tails in the front who understand the language of men.

I must confess that I had trouble accustoming myself to life aboard ship: it dances under your feet, leans a bit to the right and a bit to the left, it is hard to eat and sleep, and you step on each other's feet due to the lack of space; besides, the chained rowers stare at you with such ferocious eyes as to make you think that, if they weren't in fact chained, they would tear you to pieces in a flash: and the owner told me that sometimes it happens. On the other hand, when the wind is favorable, the sail billows out, the rowers lift their oars, and you think you are flying in an enchanted silence; you see dolphins leap out of the water, and the sailors

claim that they can discover, from the expression on their snouts, the weather we will have the next day. That ship was well plastered with pitch and yet the entire keel was riddled with holes; they were ship worms, they explained. In port, too, I had seen that all the moored ships were worm-eaten: there was nothing to be done, said the owner, who was also the captain. When the ship is old, it's broken up and burnt; but I had an idea, and the same for the anchor. It's stupid to make it out of iron; the rust devours it, and it doesn't last two years. And fishing nets? Those sailors, when the wind is good, dropped a net that had wooden floats and rocks as ballast. Rocks! If they had been lead they could have been four times less cumbersome. Of course I did not say a word to anyone, but—as you too will understand—I was already thinking of the lead I would dig out of Icnusa's entrails, and I was selling the bearskin before I had shot the bear.

We came in sight of the island after eleven days at sea. We entered a small harbor by rowing; around us there were granite cliffs and slaves who were carving columns. They were not giants and they did not sleep in their own ears; they were made like us and communicated well enough with the sailors, but their guards did not let them speak. This was a land of rocks and wind, which I liked on sight: the air was full of the smell of herbs, bitter and wild, and the people seemed strong and simple.

The land of metals was two days' walk away: I hired a donkey with a driver, and this is actually true, they are small donkeys (though not like cats, as they say on the mainland) but robust and tough; in short, in all rumors there may be some truth, perhaps a truth hidden beneath veils of words, like a riddle. For example, I saw that the story of the rock fortresses was quite correct; they are not as big as mountains, but solid, regular in shape, with hewn stones fitted together with precision. And what is curious is that everyone says that "they have always been there," and nobody knows by whom, how, why, and when they were built. That the islanders devour foreigners, however, is a great lie. Going in stages they led me to the mine without making any difficulties or indulging in mysteries, as if their land belonged to everyone.

The land of metals is enough to make you drunk, as happens when a hound enters a wood full of game and jumps from scent to scent, shivering all over and going half crazy.

It is near the sea, a line of hills which on high become rocky crags, and near and far, all the way to the horizon, one sees plumes of smoke from the foundries, surrounded by people working, free and slaves: and the story of the stone that burns is also true; I could scarcely believe my eyes. It doesn't catch fire easily, but then it produces a great deal of heat and lasts for a long time. They brought it there from God knows where, in baskets on donkeys' backs—it is black, greasy, fragile, and not very heavy.

So, as I was saying, there are marvelous stones, certainly heavy with metals never seen, which surface in white, violet, and blue streaks: beneath that land there must be a fabulous tracery of veins. I would willingly have lost myself in it, tapping, digging, and testing; but I am a Rodmund, and my rock is lead. I immediately set to work.

I found a deposit on the country's western border, where I believe nobody had ever searched: in fact, there were no pits, nor tunnels, nor heaps of rubble, and there weren't even any signs on the surface; the rocks on the surface were like all the other rocks. But just below, the lead was there: and this is a thing of which I had often thought, that we prospectors believe we find the metal with our eyes, experience, and skill, but in reality what guides is something more profound, a force like that which guides the salmon to go back up our rivers, or the swallows to return to the nest. Perhaps it happens with us as with the water diviners, who do not know what guides them to the water, but something does guide them and twists the wand in their hands.

I can't say how, but right there was the lead: I felt it under my feet, turbid, poisonous, and heavy, stretching for two miles along a brook in a wood where wild bees nest in the lightning-struck tree trunks. In a short time I had bought slaves who dug for me, and as soon as I had laid aside a bit of money I also bought myself a woman. Not just to have a good time: I chose her carefully, not looking so much for beauty but rather that she be healthy, wide in the hips, young, and merry. I chose her like that, so that she gives me a Rodmund, and our art does not perish; and I haven't been behindhand, because my hands and knees have begun to shake, and my teeth are loose in my gums and have turned blue like those of my ancestor who came from the sea. This Rodmund will be born at the end of the coming winter, in this land where palms grow, salt condenses, and at night you can hear the wild dogs baying on the track of a bear. In this village I have founded near the brook of the wild bees, and to which I would have liked to give a name in my language, which I am forgetting, Bak der Binnen, meaning "Brook of the Bees": but the people here have accepted the name only in part, and among themselves, in their language, which by now is mine, they call it Bacu Abis.

MERCURY

With my wife, Maggie, I the undersigned Corporal Abrahams have lived on this island for fourteen years. I had been sent here as garrison: it seems that on a nearby island (I mean to say "the nearest": it is northeast from this one, not less than 1,200 miles, and is called St. Helena) was exiled an important and dangerous person, and it was feared that his supporters might help him to escape and take shelter down here. This is a story which I have never believed: my island is called Desolation, and never was an island's name better chosen; so I could never understand what such an important person would come looking for here.

The rumor went around that he was a renegade, an adulterer, a Papist, rabble-rouser, and braggart. As long as he was alive, there were with us another twelve soldiers, young, merry fellows, from Wales and Surrey; they were also good farmers and gave us a hand in the work. Then the rabble-rouser died, and after that a gunboat came to take us all home: but Maggie and I remembered certain old debts and preferred to remain here to watch over our pigs. Our island has the shape you can see below.

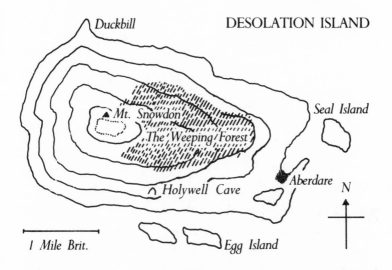

DESOLATION ISLAND

It is the loneliest island in the world. It was discovered more than once, by the Portuguese, the Dutch, and even before that by savages who carved signs and idols in the rocks of Mount Snowdon; but nobody has ever stayed on, because it rains here half the year and the soil is good only for sorghum and potatoes. Nevertheless, those who are not choosy certainly won't die of hunger, because the northern coast for five months of the year swarms with seals, and the two small islands to the south are full of seagulls' nests: all you have to do is get a boat and you can find as many eggs as you want. They taste of fish, but they are nourishing and kill your 97 hunger; everything here tastes of fish, even the potatoes and the pigs who eat them.

On the slopes east of Snowdon grow holm oaks and other trees whose names I do not know: in the autumn they bloom with light blue, fleshy flowers that smell like unwashed people; in the winter, hard, sour berries, not good to eat. They are strange trees: they suck up water from the deep earth and throw it up in rain from the tops of their branches; even on dry days, the land beneath this forest is humid. The water that pours down from the branches is good to drink, and indeed has a soothing effect on inflammations, although it tastes of moss: we gather it with a system of gutters and basins. This forest, which, in fact, is the only one on the island, we called the Weeping Forest.

We live at Aberdare. It is not a town—there are only four wooden huts, two of which are caved in; but one of the Welshmen insisted on calling it that, since he himself came from Aberdare. Duckbill is the island's northernmost point: the soldier Cochrane, who suffered from homesickness, went there often and spent whole days amid the salty mist and wind because it seemed to him that he was closer to England. (He also built a beacon there, which nobody ever bothered to light.) It is called Duckbill because, when seen from the east, it really has the shape of a duck's bill.

Seal Island is flat and sandy; the seals go there in the winter to have their pups. Holywell Cave was given that name by my wife, and I don't know what she saw in it. At certain periods, when we were alone, she went there almost every night, with a torch, even though it was almost two miles from Aberdare. She would sit there to spin or knit, waiting for God knows what. I asked her about it more than once: she told me some confused things, that she heard voices and saw shadows, and that down there, where not even the thunder of the sea reached, she felt less alone and more protected.

I, however, feared that Maggie was leaning toward idolatry. In that cave there were boulders that looked like figures of men and animals; one boulder, right in the back, was a horned skull. Certainly these shapes were not made by human hands: and so who did them? I, on my account, preferred to give them a wide berth; also because in the cave one sometimes heard stifled rumbles, like attacks of colic in the earth's entrails, the floor was hot under your feet, and from certain fissures in the back came jets of steam with a sulfurous smell. In short, I would have given an entirely different name to that cave: but Maggie said that the voice she claimed to hear would one day pronounce our fate, and the island's and all humanity's.

Maggie and I remained alone for several years; each year, at Easter, Burton's whaler would pass by bringing news of the world and provisions and take on the small amount of smoked pork that we had produced; but then everything changed. Three years ago Burton set ashore here two Dutchmen: Willem was still nearly a child, shy, blond, and pink-skinned; on his forehead he had a silvery sore which looked like leprosy and no ship wanted him aboard. Hendrik was older; he was thin and had gray hair and a wrinkled brow: he told a not very clear story of a brawl in which he supposedly bashed in his quartermaster's head, and the gallows was waiting for him in Holland; but he did not speak like a sailor and had gentleman's hands, not the hands of someone who bashes in heads. One morning a few months later we saw smoke rise from one of the Egg Islands. I took the boat and went over to look. I found two shipwrecked Italians, Gaetano of Amalfi and Andrea of Noli. Their ship had split on the Plowshare rocks, and they had swum to safety; they did not know that the large island was inhabited; they had lit a fire of brushwood and guano to dry off. I 99 told them that in a few months Burton would pass by again and he could land them in Europe, but they refused with terror. After what they had seen that night, never again would they set foot on a ship; and it took a great deal of persuading on my part to convince them to come on my small boat and cross the hundred yards of sea that separated us from Desolation. As far as they were concerned, they would have stayed on that miserable rock eating seagulls' eggs until their natural death.

Not that Desolation lacks for space. I put up the four men in one of the huts abandoned by the Welshmen; they had quite enough room, also because their luggage was modest. Only Hendrik had a wooden trunk, closed with a lock. Willem's sore was not leprosy at all; Maggie cured it in a few weeks with compresses of an herb she knows——it is not actually watercress, it's a succulent herb which grows at the borders of the forest and is good to eat, even if then it gives you strange dreams: but we call it watercress. To tell the truth, she did not only treat him with compresses: she shut herself up with him in the bedroom and sang him chants like lullabies, with pauses that seemed to me too long. I was glad and less worried when Willem was cured, but immediately after began another annoying business with Hendrik. He and Maggie took long walks together, and I heard them talk about the seven keys, Hermes Trismegistus, the union of contraries, and other rather obscure matters. Hendrik built himself a sturdy hut without windows, put his trunk in it, and spent whole days there, sometimes with Maggie: you could see smoke rising out of the chimney. They would also go to the cave and return with colored stones, which Hendrik called "cinnabars."

The two Italians worried me less. They too looked at Maggie with shining eyes, but they did not know English and could not talk with her. What's more, they were jealous of each other and spent their days keeping an eye on each other. Andrea was very devout, and in a short time had filled the island with saints made of wood and baked clay: he had given a terracotta Madonna as a gift to Maggie, who, however, did not know what to do with it and put it in a corner of the kitchen. In short, it would have been clear to anyone that these four men needed four women. One day I brought them all together and without beating around the bush told them that if one of them touched Maggie he would end up in Hell, because one should not lust after another man's woman: but I would send him there myself, at the cost of ending up there too. When Burton came by again, with his hold brimming with whale oil, all of us in agreement solemnly commissioned him with the task of finding four wives, but he laughed in our faces. What did we think? That it was easy to find women ready to settle down among the seals, on this forgotten island, to marry four good-for-nothings? Perhaps if we paid them, but with what? Certainly not with our sausages, half pig and half seal, which stank of fish more than his whaler. He left and immediately after hoisted his sails.

That very evening, just before nightfall, we heard a great rumble of thunder, as though the island itself was being shaken to its roots. In a few minutes the sky darkened and the black cloud that covered it was lit from below as by a fire. From the top of Mount Snowdon we saw first rapid red flashes leap out and climb up into the sky, then a broad, slow stream of burning lava: it did not descend toward us but to the left, the south, pouring from ridge to ridge, hissing and crackling. After an hour it reached the sea and there it was doused with a roar, lifting up a column of vapor. None of us had ever thought that Mount Snowdon could be a volcano; and yet the shape of its summit, with a round hollow at least two hundred feet deep, could have made us suspect this.

The spectacle continued all through the night, calming down

every so often, then picking up again with a new series of explosions; it seemed that it would never end. Yet, toward dawn, a hot wind blew from the east, the sky cleared off again, and the uproar gradually died down until it was reduced to a murmur, then silence. The mantle of lava, which had been yellow and dazzling, turned reddish like smoldering coals, and by daylight it was extinguished.

My preoccupation was the pigs. I told Maggie that she should go to sleep, and asked the four men to come with me; I wanted to see what had changed on the island.

, Nothing had happened to the pigs, but they ran to meet us like brothers (I can't stand people who speak badly of pigs: they are animals who are quite conscious, and it pains me when I have to slaughter them). On the northeastern slope several cracks had opened, two large ones whose bottoms cannot be seen. The southwestern edge of the Weeping Forest was buried, and the strip alongside for a breadth of two hundred feet was dried out and had caught fire; the earth must have been hotter than the sky, because the fire followed the trunks all the way to the roots, scooping out passages where they had been. The mantle of lava was all dotted with burst bubbles with edges as sharp as splinters of glass, and it looked like a gigantic cheese grater: it issued from the southern lip of the crater, which had collapsed, while the northern lip, which formed the top of the mountain, was now a rounded crest that seemed much higher than before.

When we looked into the Holywell Cave we were petrified with astonishment. It was another cave, completely different, as when one shuffles a deck of cards—narrow where before it had been broad, high where it had been low: at one point the ceiling had

collapsed and the stalactites instead of pointing down now pointed sideways, like storks' beaks. At the rear, where before there had been the Devil's Skull, there was now an enormous chamber, like the dome of a church, still full of smoke and crackling sounds, so much so that Andrea and Gaetano wanted at all costs to turn back. I sent them to call Maggie so that she too would come and see her cave, and, as I expected, Maggie arrived gasping from the run and emotion, and the two Italians stayed outside, presumably to pray to their saints and to say their litanies. Inside the cave Maggie ran back and forth like a hunting dog, as if those voices she said she heard were calling to her; suddenly she let out a scream which made all our hairs stand on end. There was in the sky of the cupola a crack, and drops were falling from it, but not of water: shiny, heavy drops, which plunked on the rock floor and burst into a thousand spattering drops that rolled far away. A little lower down a pool had formed, and then we understood that it was mercury: Hendrik touched it, and I did too: it was a cold, lively material, which moved in small, irritated, and frenetic waves.

Hendrik seemed transfigured. He exchanged swift glances with Maggie whose significance I could not catch, and he said some obscure, mixed-up things to us, which, however, she seemed to understand: that it was time to initiate the Great Work; that, like the sky, the earth too has its dew; that the cave was full of the spiritus mundi. Then he turned openly to Maggie and said to her: "Come here this evening; we will make the beast with two backs." He took from his neck a chain with a bronze cross and showed it to us: on the cross a snake was crucified, and he threw the cross on the mercury in the pool, and the cross floated.

If you looked around, mercury was oozing from all the cracks of the new cave, like beer from new vats. If you listened you heard a sonorous murmur, produced by thousands of metallic droplets which fell from the cave's vault and splattered on the ground, and by the sound of the trickles vibrating, like melted silver, before sinking in the crevices in the rock floor.

To tell the truth, I had never liked Hendrik—of the four men, he was the one I liked the least; but at that moment he filled me with fear, rage, and revulsion. He had a crooked, fleeting light in his eyes, like that of mercury; it seemed that he had turned into mercury, that it was running in his veins and shone through his eyes. He scurried about the cave like a ferret, dragging Maggie by the wrist, plunging his hands into the pools of mercury, spraying it over himself and pouring it on his head, as a thirsty man would do with water: one step more and he might have drunk it. Maggie followed him, spellbound. I stood it for a while, then I flipped open my knife, grabbed him by the chest, and pushed him against the rock wall: I am much stronger than he is, and he went slack like a sail when the wind drops. I wanted to know who he was, what he wanted of us and the island, and what about that business of the beast with two backs.

He looked like a man who has awakened from a dream, and he spoke out right away. He confessed that the story of the murdered quartermaster was a lie, but not that of the gallows that awaited him in Holland: he had proposed to the States General to transform the sand of the dunes into gold, had obtained a fund of one hundred thousand florins, and had spent a few of them in experiments and the rest in riotous living, then he had been asked to execute before the judges what he called the experimentum crucis; but from a thousand pounds of sand he had succeeded in obtaining only two flakes of gold, so he had jumped from the window, had hidden in his girlfriend's house, and then had embarked secretly on the first ship leaving for the Cape. He had in his trunk his alchemist's paraphernalia. As for the beast, he said it was not something that could be explained in a few words. Mercury, for their work, would be indispensable, because it is a fixed volatile spirit, that is, the female principle, and combined with sulfur, which is hot male earth, permits you to obtain the philosophic Egg, which is precisely the Beast with Two Backs, for in it are united and commingled male and female. Quite a tale this was, clear, straight talk, truly that of an alchemist, of which I didn't believe a word. The two of them, he and Maggie, were the beast with two backs: he gray and hairy, she white and smooth, inside the cave or God knows where, or perhaps in our very own bed while I was taking care of the pigs; they were preparing to do it, drunk with the mercury as they were, if they hadn't done it already.

Perhaps the mercury was already coursing through my veins too, for at that moment I was really seeing red. After twenty years of marriage, Maggie didn't mean all that much to me, but at that moment I was burning with desire for her and would have murdered for her. But I managed to control myself; indeed, I was still holding Hendrik tightly pressed against the wall when I got an idea, and I asked him how much mercury was worth: he, with his craft, ought to know that.

"Twelve English guineas a pound," he replied in a whisper.

"Swear!"

"I swear," he replied, lifting up his two thumbs and spitting on the ground between them; perhaps it was their way of swearing, these transmuters of metals: but he had my knife so close to his throat that certainly he was telling the truth. I let him go, and he, still completely terrified, explained to me that raw mercury like ours is not worth much, but that it can be purified by distilling it, like whiskey, in cast-iron or terracotta retorts; then the retort is broken and in the residue you find lead, often silver, and sometimes gold; that this was their secret; but he would do it for me if I promised to spare his life.

I promised absolutely nothing and instead told him that with the mercury I wanted to pay for the four wives. Making clay retorts and jars must surely be easier than changing the sand of Holland into gold: so get cracking, since Easter was approaching and so also Burton's visit. I wanted to have ready for Easter forty pint jars of purified mercury, all the same, each with a fine cover, smooth and round, since the eye wants its share too. He should get help also from the other three, and I too would give him a hand. He needn't worry about the baking of retorts and jars: there already was the furnace in which Andrea baked his saints.

I learned how to distill immediately, and in ten days the jars were ready: they were for a single pint, but each pint of mercury weighed seventeen abundant pounds, so heavy that it was hard to lift one with your outstretched arms, and when you shook one it seemed that inside writhed a living animal. As for finding the crude mercury, that was a cinch: in the cave you wallowed in mercury, it dripped on your head and shoulders, and when you went home you found it in your pockets, your boots, even in the bed, and it went a bit to everyone's head, so much so that it began to seem natural to us that we should exchange it for some women. It is truly a bizarre substance: it is cold and elusive, always restless, but when it is quite still you can see yourself in it better than in a mirror. If you stir it around in a bowl it continues to twirl for almost half an hour. Not only does Hendrik's sacrilegious crucifix float on it but also stones, even lead. Not gold: Maggie tried it with her ring, but it immediately sank to the bottom, and when we fished it up again it had turned into tin. In short, it is a material I do not like, and I was in a hurry to close the deal and get rid of it.

At Easter, Burton arrived, carried off the forty jars carefully sealed with wax and clay, and left without making any promises. One evening toward the end of autumn we saw his sail loom up in the rain, grow larger, and then disappear in the murky air and darkness. We thought he was waiting for the light to enter the small anchorage, as he usually did, but in the morning there was no trace of Burton or his whaling ship. There were instead, standing on the beach, drenched and stiff with the cold, four women plus two children, all clustered tightly together in a heap due to cold and shyness; one of them silently delivered a letter from Burton. A few lines—that to find four women for four unknowns on a desolate island, he had had to hand over all the mercury and nothing had been left for the brokerage; that he would claim it, in mercury and smoked pork, to the tune of 10 percent on his next visit; that they weren't first-choice women, but he had not found anything better; that he preferred to land them quickly and return to his whaler to avoid witnessing disgusting brawls and because he was neither a go-between nor a pimp, nor even a priest to officiate at a wedding; that nevertheless he advised us to perform the weddings ourselves, as best we could, for the health of our souls, which at any rate he already considered somewhat ailing.

I called out the four men and wanted to propose that we draw lots, but I immediately saw that there was no need for that. There was a middle-aged mulatto, plumpish, with a scar on her forehead, who stared insistently at Willem, and Willem looked at her with curiosity: the woman could have been his mother. I said to Willem: "Do you want her? Take her!"——he took her and I married them as best I could; that is, I asked her if she wanted him and him if he wanted her, but the little speech about "for rich or poor, in sickness or in health" I could not recall exactly and so I invented it there and then, winding up with "until death overtakes 107 you," which seemed to me to have a good sound. I was just finishing up with these two when I saw that Gaetano had chosen a young, one-eyed girl, or perhaps she had chosen him, and they were running away together in the rain, holding hands, so much so that I had to pursue them and marry them from a distance as I too was running. Of the two who remained, Andrea took a black woman about thirty, pretty and even elegant, with a plumed hat and a boa of ostrich feathers that was dripping wet, but with a rather equivocal manner, and I married them too, although I was still gasping for breath because of the race I had just run.

Hendrik was left and a small, thin girl who was in fact the mother of the two children. She had gray eyes and looked around her as though the scene did not concern her but amused her. She was not looking at Hendrik but was looking at me; Hendrik was looking at Maggie, who had just come out of the hut and had not taken out her curlers, and Maggie was looking at Hendrik. Then it popped into my head that the two children could help me take care of the pigs; Maggie would certainly not give me children; that Hendrik and Maggie would get along very well together, making the beast with two backs and their distillations; and that the girl with the gray eyes did not displease me, even if she was much younger than I; on the contrary, she made me feel gay and light-hearted, like a tickle, and brought to mind the idea of catching her on the wing like a butterfly. So I asked her her name and then I asked myself in a loud voice, in the presence of witnesses: "Do you wish, Corporal Daniel K. Abrahams, to take as wife the here present Rebecca Johnson?" and I answered myself yes, and since the girl too was agreed, we got married.

PHOSPHORUS

In June 1942 I spoke frankly to the lieutenant and the director: I realized that my work was becoming useless, and they too realized this and advised me to look for another job, in one of the not too many niches the law still granted me.

I was futilely looking when one morning, a very rare event, I was called to the mine's telephone: from the other end of the line a Milanese voice, which seemed to me crude and energetic, and which said that it belonged to a Dr. Martini, summoned me to an appointment on the following Sunday at the Hotel Suisse in Turin, without vouchsafing me the luxury of any details. But he had said "Hotel Suisse" and not "Albergo Svizzera" as a loyal citizen would be obliged to say: at that time, which was the time of Starace,* one was very attentive to such piddling details, and one's ears were expert at intercepting certain nuances.

In the foyer (oh, pardon me, in the lobby, which isn't a French word) of the Hotel Suisse, an anachronistic oasis of plush upholstery, velvets, shadows, and draperies, Dr. Martini, who was prevalently a *commendatore*, as I had learned just before from the doorman, was waiting for me. He was a thickset man of about sixty, of medium height, tanned, almost bald: his face had heavy features, but his eyes were small and astute, and his mouth, a trifle twisted to the left as in a grimace of contempt, was thin as a cut. This *commendatore* revealed himself from his first remarks to be also a no-nonsense, all-business type; and I understood at that point that this strange haste of "Aryan" Italians in dealing with Jews was not accidental. Whether intuition or calculation, it served a purpose: with a Jew, at a time of the Defense of the Race, one could be polite, one could even help him, and even boast (cautiously) about having helped him, but it was not advisable to have human relations with him, nor to compromise oneself too deeply, so as not to be forced later to offer understanding or compassion.

The *commendatore* asked only a few questions, responded evasively to my many questions, and proved to be a very down-to-earth person on two fundamental points: the starting salary that he offered me came to a sum that I would never have dared ask for, and left me dumbfounded; his industry was Swiss, indeed he himself was a Swiss (he pronounced it "Sviss"), so for my possible hiring there was no difficulty. I found strange—in fact, frankly comic—his Swiss-ism expressed in such a virulent Milanese accent; I found, however, his many reticences quite justifiable.

The factory of which he was the owner and director was on the outskirts of Milan, and I would have to move to Milan. It

*A. Starace was for many years secretary of the Fascist National Party. He distinguished himself by the stupid zeal with which he strove to "purify" the customs of the Italians, combating the use of foreign words (in fact, such words as "hotel" or "foyer").

produced hormonal extracts: I, however, would have to deal with a very precise problem, that is, research into a new cure for diabetes which would be effective if taken orally. Did I know anything about diabetes? Not much, I replied, but my maternal grandfather had died of diabetes, and also on my paternal side several of my uncles, legendary devourers of pasta, had shown symptoms of the disease in their old age. Hearing this, the *commendatore* became more attentive and his eyes smaller: I realized later that, since the tendency to diabetes is hereditary, it would not have displeased him to have at his disposal an authentic diabetic, of a basically human race, on whom he could test certain of his ideas and preparations. He told me that the offered salary was subject to rapid raises; that the laboratory was modern, well equipped, and spacious; that in the factory there was a library with more than ten thousand volumes; and, finally, like a magician extracting a rabbit from his tall silk hat, he added that, perhaps I did not know it (and indeed I didn't), but already working in his laboratory, and on the same problem, was a person I knew well, a classmate of mine and a friend, who in fact had spoken of me: Giulia Vineis. I should decide with calm: I would find him at the Hotel Suisse two Sundays from today.

The very next day I quit the mine and moved to Milan with the few things I felt were indispensable: my bike, Rabelais, the *Macaronaeae*, *Moby Dick* translated by Pavese, a few other books, my pickax, climbing rope, logarithmic ruler, and recorder.

The *commendatore*'s lab was not inferior to his description of it: a palace in comparison to the mine's lab. I found already set out for my arrival a workbench, a ventilation hood, a desk, a closet filled with glassware, and an inhuman silence and orderliness. "My" glassware was countersigned with a small dot in blue enamel glaze, so that it would not be confused with glassware from other closets, and also because "here with us breakages have to be paid for." This, at any event, was only one of the many regulations that the *commendatore* had transmitted to me on the day of my arrival: he passed them off to me as examples of "Swiss precision," the soul of the laboratory and the entire factory, but to me they seemed a collection of witless impediments bordering on persecution mania.

The *commendatore* explained to me that the factory's work, particulary the problem he had entrusted to me, had to be attentively protected from possible industrial spies. These spies could be outsiders but also clerks and workers in the factory itself, despite all the precautions he used in hiring. Therefore I must not talk with anyone about the subject that had been proposed to me, nor of its possible developments: not even with my colleagues, in fact with them even less than with others. For this reason, every clerk had his particular schedule of hours, which coincided with a single pair of tram runs coming from the city: A had to come in at 8, B at 8:04, C at 8:08, and so on, and the same for quitting times, in such a manner that never would two colleagues have the opportunity to travel in the same tramcar. For people who came to work late and for those who left before quitting time there were heavy fines.

The last hour of the day, even if the world came to an end, must be dedicated to dismantling, washing, and putting away the glassware, so that no one entering outside the lab hours could reconstruct what work had been done during the day. Every evening a daily report must be compiled and handed in in a sealed envelope to him personally or to Signora Loredana, who was his secretary.

I could eat lunch where I wished; it was not his intention to sequester the clerks in the factory during the midday break. However, he told me (and here his mouth twisted more than usual and became even thinner) there were no good cheap *trattorie* thereabouts, and his advice was to equip myself for lunching in the lab; if I brought the raw materials from home, a worker there would see to cooking it for me.

As for the library, the regulations that had to be followed were singularly severe. Books could not be taken out of the factory under any circumstances; they could be consulted only with the consent of the librarian, Signorina Paglietta. Underlining a word, or just making a mark with pen or pencil, was a very serious offense: Paglietta was expected to check every book, page by page, when returned, and if she found a mark, the book had to be destroyed and replaced at the expense of the culprit. It was forbidden even to leave between the sheets a bookmark, or turn down the corner of a page: "someone" could have drawn clues from this about the factory's interests and activities—in short, violate its secret. Within this system, it is logical that keys were fundamental: in the evening, everything had to be locked up, even the analytical balance, and the keys then deposited with the custodian. The *commendatore* had a key that opened all the locks.

This viaticum of precepts and prohibitions would have made me permanently unhappy if on entering the lab I had not found Giulia Vineis, quite calm, seated beside her workbench. She was not working—instead she was darning her stockings, and seemed to be waiting for me. She greeted me with affectionate familiarity and a meaningful grimace.

We had been classmates at the university for four years, and had attended together all the lab courses, which are wonderful matchmakers, without ever becoming particular friends. Giulia was a dark girl, minute and quick; she had eyebrows with an elegant arc, a smooth, pointed face, a lively but precise way of moving. She was more open to practice than to theory, full of human warmth, Catholic without rigidity, generous and slap-dash; she spoke in a veiled, distracted voice, as if she were definitely tired of living, which she was not at all. She had been there for nearly a year—yes, she was the person who mentioned my name to the *commendatore*: she knew vaguely about my precarious situation at the mine, thought that I would be well suited for that research work, and besides, why not admit it, she was fed up with being alone. But I shouldn't get any ideas: she was engaged, very much engaged, a complicated and tumultuous business that she would explain to me later. And what about me? No? No girls? That's bad: she would try to help me out there, forget the racial laws; a lot of nonsense anyway, what importance could they have?

She advised me not to take the *commendatore*'s strange ideas too seriously. Giulia was one of those people who, apparently without asking questions or going to any trouble, immediately knew everything about everybody, which to me, God knows why, never happens; so she was for me a tourist guide and a first-class interpreter. In a single session she taught me the essentials, the pulley-lines hidden behind the factory's scenery and the roles of the main characters. The *commendatore* was the boss, although subjected to obscure other bosses in Basel; however, the person who gave the orders was Loredana (and she pointed her out to me from the window on the courtyard: tall, brunette, shapely, rather vulgar, a bit faded), who was his secretary and mistress. They had a villa on the lake, and he— "who was old but horny"—took her sailing. There were photos of this in the main office, hadn't I seen them? Also Signor Grasso, in the Personnel Office, was after Loredana, but for the moment she, Giulia, had not yet been able to ascertain whether he'd already been to bed with her or not: she would keep me posted. Living in that factory was not difficult; it was difficult to work there because of all those entanglements. The solution was simple—just don't work: she had realized this immediately, and in a year, modesty aside, she had done hardly anything—all that she did was set up the apparatus in the morning, just enough to satisfy the eye, and dismount it in the evening in accordance with regulations. The daily report she created out of her imagination. Apart from that, she prepared her trousseau, slept a great deal, wrote torrential letters to her fiancé, and, against regulations, started conversations with everyone who came within earshot: with Ambrogio, half dazed, who took care of the rabbits for the experiments; with Michela, who watched over the keys and probably was a Fascist spy; with Varisco, the woman worker who, according to the *commendatore*, was supposed to prepare my lunch; with Maiocchi, a fighter on Franco's side in Spain, pomaded and a womanizer; and, impartially, with
Moioli, pallid and gelatinous, who had nine children, had been a

member of the People's Party, and whose back the Fascists had broken with their clubs.

Varisco, she explained, was her creature: she was attached and devoted and did everything she was ordered to do, including certain expeditions into the department for the production of organo-therapeutics (forbidden to those not working there), from which she returned with livers, brains, suprarenal capsules, and other rare innards. Varisco was also engaged, and between the two of them there was profound solidarity and an intense exchange of intimate confidences. From Varisco, who, since she was in charge of cleaning, had access to all departments, she had found out that production too was enveloped in closely meshed anti-spy trappings: all pipes for water, vapor, vacuum, gas, naphtha, etc., ran in underground passages or were sheathed in cement, and only the valves were accessible; the machines were covered with complicated gear-cases and locked. The dials of the thermometers and manometers were not graduated; they bore only conventional colored marks.

Of course, if I wanted to work and the research into diabetes interested me, go right ahead and do it, we would be friends anyway; but I shouldn't count on her collaboration because she had other things to think about. I could, however, count on her and Varisco when it came to cooking. They, both of them, had to start training, in view of their coming marriages, and so they would offer me some feeds which would make me forget all about ration cards and rationing. It did not seem to me rule-abiding that complicated feats of cuisine should take place in the lab, but Giulia told me that in that laboratory, outside of a certain mysterious consultant from Basel who seemed mummified, came once a month (in any case, abundantly preannounced), looked around as though he were in a museum, and left without breathing a word, no living being ever entered, and you could do whatever you liked, so long as you left no traces behind. In the memory of man, the *commendatore* had never set foot there.

A few days after I was hired, the *commendatore* summoned me to the main office, and on that occasion I noticed that the photos of the sailboat—actually very chaste—were really there. He told me that the moment had come to begin the real work. The first thing I had to do was go to the library, ask Paglietta for the Kerrn, a treatise on diabetes. I knew German, didn't I? Good, so I could read it in the original text and not in a very poor French translation which the people in Basel had commissioned. He, he admitted, had read only the latter, without understanding much of it, but nevertheless gaining from it the conviction that Dr. Kerrn was a fellow who knew plenty and that it would be wonderful to be the first to translate his ideas into practice: certainly, he wrote in a rather involuted manner, but the people in Basel were very keen on this business of an oral anti-diabetic, especially the mummified consultant, so I should get Kerrn, read him attentively, and then we would discuss it. But meanwhile, so as not to waste time, I could begin work. His many preoccupations had not allowed him to devote to the text the attention it deserved, but he had nonetheless gotten from it two fundamental ideas, and we should try to test them in practice.

The first idea concerned anthocyanins. Anthocyanins, as you know very well, are the pigments of red and blue flowers: they are substances easy to oxidize and deoxidize, as is also glucose, and diabetes is an anomaly in the oxidizing of glucose: "hence," with the anthocyanins one could try to reestablish a normal oxidizing of glucose. The petals of the cornflower are very rich in anthocyanins; in view of the problem, he had put a whole field under cultivation with cornflowers and had the petals harvested and dried in the sun: I should try to make extracts from them, administer them to rabbits, and check their glycemia.

The second idea was just as vague, and at once simplistic and complicated. Still according to Dr. Kerrn, in the *commendatore*'s Lombardian interpretation, phosphoric acid had a fundamental importance in the metabolism of carbohydrates: and up to this point there was nothing to object to; less convincing was the hypothesis elaborated by the *commendatore* himself on Kerrn's rather misty fundamentals, namely, that it would suffice to administer to the diabetic a little phosphorus of vegetal origin to correct his subverted metabolism. At that time I was so young as to think that it might be possible to change a superior's ideas; therefore I put forth two or three objections, but I saw immediately that under their blows the *commendatore* hardened like a sheet of copper under a hammer. He cut me short and, with a certain peremptory tone of his that transformed his suggestions into commands, advised me to analyze a good number of plants, select the richest in organic phosphorus, make from them the usual extracts, and stick them into the usual rabbits. Enjoy your work and good afternoon.

When I told Giulia about the outcome of this colloquy, her judgment was immediate and angry: the old man is crazy. But I had provoked him, descending to his level and showing him from the start that I took him seriously: I'd asked for it, and I should see now what I could do with those cornflowers, phosphorus, and rabbits. In her opinion, that mania of mine about work, which even went to the point of prostituting myself to the *commendatore*'s senile fairy tales, resulted from the fact that I didn't have a girl friend: if I had one, I would have thought about her instead of anthocyanins. It was truly a pity that she, Giulia, was not available, because she realized the sort of person I was, one of those who do not take the initiative, indeed run away, and must be led by the hand, solving little by little all their complicated conflicts. Well, in Milan there was a cousin of hers, also rather shy; she would arrange for me to meet her. But what the deuce, I too, by heavens, should get busy; it hurt her heart to see someone like me throw away the best years of his youth on rabbits. This Giulia was a bit of a witch—she read palms, went to mediums, and had premonitory dreams—and sometimes I have dared to think that this haste of hers to free me of an old anguish and procure for me immediately a modest *117* portion of joy came from a dark intuition of hers about what fate had in store for me, and was unconsciously aimed at deflecting it.

We went together to see the movie *Port of Shadows* and thought it marvelous, and we confessed to each other that we'd identified with the main actors: slim, dark Giulia with the ethereal Michèle Morgan and her ice-green eyes, and I, mild and recessive, with the deserter Jean Gabin, a fascinator and tough guy, killed dead—ridiculous, and besides, those two loved each other and we didn't, right?

When the movie was about to end, Giulia announced that I would have to take her home. I had to go to the dentist, but Giulia said: "If you don't take me, I'll yell, 'Get your hands off me, you pig!' " I tried to object, but Giulia took a deep breath and in the darkness of the movie house began, "Get your . . .": so I phoned the dentist and took her home.

Giulia was a lioness, capable of traveling for ten hours standing up in a train packed with people running away from the bombings to spend two hours with her man, happy and radiant if she could engage in a violent verbal duel with the *commendatore* or Loredana, but she was afraid of insects and thunder. She called me to evict a tiny spider from her workbench (I wasn't allowed to kill it, but had to put it in a weighing bottle and carry it outside to the flowerbed), and this made me feel virtuous and strong like Hercules faced by the Hydra of Lerna, and at the same time tempted, since I perceived the intense feminine charge in the request. A furious storm broke, Giulia stood fast for two strokes of lightning and at the third ran to me for shelter. I felt the warmth of her body against mine, dizzying and new, familiar in dreams, but I did not return her embrace; if I had done so, perhaps her destiny and mine would have gone with a crash off the rails, toward a common, completely unpredictable future.

The librarian, whom I had never seen before, presided over the library like a watchdog, one of those poor dogs who are deliberately made vicious by being chained up and given little to eat; or better, like the old, toothless cobra, pale because of centuries of darkness, who guards the king's treasure in the *Jungle Book*. Paglietta, poor woman, was little less than a *lusus naturae*: she was small, without breasts or hips, waxen, wilted, and monstrously myopic: she wore glasses so thick and concave that, looking at her head-on, her eyes, light blue, almost white, seemed very far away, stuck at the back of her cranium. She gave the impression of never having been young, although she was certainly not more than thirty, and of having been born there, in the shadows, in that vague odor of mildew and stale air. Nobody knew anything about her, the *commendatore* himself talked about her with irritated impatience, and Giulia admitted that she hated her instinctively, without knowing why, without pity, as a fox hates a dog. She said that she stank of mothballs and looked constipated. Paglietta asked me why I wanted the Kerrn in particular, insisted on seeing my identity card, inspected it with a malevolent air, made me sign a register, and reluctantly surrendered the book.

It was a strange book: it would be hard to think of its being written and published in any other place than the Third Reich. The author was not without a certain ability, but every one of his pages gave off the arrogance of someone who knows that his statements will not be disputed. He wrote, indeed harangued, like a possessed prophet, as though the metabolism of glucose, in the diabetic and the healthy person, had been revealed to him by Jehovah on Sinai or, rather, by Wotan on Valhalla. Perhaps wrongly, I immediately conceived for Kerrn's theories a resentful distrust; but I have not heard that the thirty years that have passed since then have led to their reevaluation.

The adventure of the anthocyanins soon ended. It had begun with a picturesque invasion of cornflowers, sacks upon sacks of delicate pale blue petals, dry and fragile like tiny potato chips. They produced extracts of changeable colors, also picturesque, but extremely unstable: after a few days' attempts, still before having recourse to the rabbits, I received from the *commendatore* the authorization to file the whole subject away. I continued to find it strange that this man, a Swiss with his feet on the ground, had let himself be convinced by that fanatical visionary, and when I got the chance, I cautiously hinted at my opinion, but he answered quite brutally that it was not for me to criticize the professors. He made it clear to me that I wasn't paid to do nothing, and urged me not to waste time but begin immediately with the phosphorus: he was convinced that the phosphorus would certainly lead us to a brilliant solution. So on to the phosphorus.

I set to work, not at all convinced, though convinced that the *commendatore*, and most likely Kerrn himself, had given in to the cheap spell of names and clichés; in fact, phosphorus has a very beautiful name (it means "bringer of light"), it is phosphores-cent, it's in the brain, it's also in fish, and *therefore* eating fish makes you intelligent; without phosophorus plants do not grow; Falières developed phosphatine, glycerophosphates for anemic children one hundred years ago; it is in the tips of matches, and girls driven desperate by love ate them to commit suicide; it is in will-o'-the-wisps, putrid flames fleeing before the wayfarer. No, it is not an emotionally neutral element: it was understandable that a Professor Kerrn, half biochemist and half witch doctor, in the environment impregnated with black magic of the Nazi court, had designated it as a medicament.

Unknown hands left on my bench at night all sorts of plants, a species a day; they were all singularly domestic plants, and I do not know how they had been chosen: onion, garlic, carrot, burdock, blueberry, yarrow milfoil, willow, garden sage, rose-mary, dog rose, juniper. I, day by day, determined their inor-ganic and total phosphorus content, and I felt like the donkey tied to a bucket pump. Just as much as the analysis of nickel in the rock had exalted me, elemental in my previous incarnation, so was I humiliated now by the daily dosage of phosphorus, because to do work in which one does not believe is a great affliction; the presence of Giulia in the next room barely did anything to cheer me up, singing in a muted voice "it's spring, wake up," and cooking away with the thermometer in the pretty little Pyrex beakers. Every so often she came to contemplate my work, provocative and mocking.

We had noticed, Giulia and I, that the same unknown hands left in the lab, in our absence, barely perceptible signs. A closet, locked in the evening, was open in the morning. A stand had changed places. The hood, left open, had been lowered. One rainy morning, like Robinson Crusoe, we found on the tile floor the print of a rubber sole: the *commendatore* wore shoes with rubber soles. "He comes at night to make love with Loredana," Giulia decided; I thought instead that that lab, obsessively tidy, must be used for some other impalpable secret Swiss activity. Systematically we stuck toothpicks on the inside part of the doors, always locked by key, which led from the Production Department into the laboratory: every morning the toothpicks had fallen out.

After two months I had about forty analyses: the plants with a higher phosphorus content were sage, celandine, and parsley. I was thinking at this point that it would be a good idea to determine in what form the phosphorus was bound, and try to isolate the phosphoric component, but the *commendatore* called Basel and then declared that there wasn't time for such subtleties: continue with the extracts, done without too much fuss, with hot water and the press, and then concentrated under vacuum: stick them into the rabbits' esophaguses and measure their glycemia.

Rabbits are not attractive animals. They are among the mammals most distant from man, perhaps because their qualities are those of humanity when humiliated and outcast: they are timid, silent, and evasive, and all they know is food and sex. Except for some country cat in my distant childhood, I never had touched an animal, and faced with the rabbits I felt a distinct revulsion: Giulia had the same reaction. Luckily, however, Varisco was on intimate terms both with the little beasts and with Ambrogio, who took care of them. She showed us that, in a drawer, there was a small assortment of appropriate instruments; there was a tall narrow box without a cover: she explained that rabbits like to hide in a den, a small space, and if one takes them by the ears (which are their natural handle) and sticks them in a box, they feel safer and stop moving. There was a rubber sound and a small wooden spindle with a transverse hole: you had to force the spindle between the animal's teeth, and then, through the hole, slip the sound down the throat quite firmly, pushing it down until you could feel it touch the bottom of the stomach; if you don't use the wood, the rabbit cuts the sound with his teeth, swallows it, and dies. Through the sound it was easy to inject the extracts into the stomach, using an ordinary syringe.

Then you have to measure the glycemia. What the tail is to mice, the ears are to rabbits, also in this instance: they have thick, prominent veins, which immediately become swollen if the ears are rubbed. From these veins, perforated by a needle, you take a drop of blood, and, without asking any questions about the various manipulations, you proceed according to Crecelius-Seifert. The rabbits either are stoic or not very sensitive to pain: none of these abuses seemed to make them suffer—as soon as they were freed and put back in the cage they calmly returned to munching on the hay, and the next time they did not show any fear. After a month I could have performed the glycemia test with my eyes closed, but it did not seem to me that our phosphorus had any effect; only one of the rabbits reacted to the extract of celandine with a lowering of its glycemia, but a few weeks later a big tumor grew on its neck. The *commendatore* told me to operate on it—I operated, with a bitter sense of guilt and vehement disgust, and it died.

Those rabbits, by order of the *commendatore*, lived each in its own cage, males and females, in strict celibacy. But there was a night bombing which, without causing many other damages, bashed all the cages, and in the morning we found the rabbits intent on a meticulous and general campaign of copulation: the bombs had not frightened them at all. When set free they had immediately dug in the flowerbeds the tunnels from which they derive their names,* and at the slightest alarm broke off their nuptials halfway through and ran for shelter. Ambrogio had a hard time rounding them up and shutting them in new cages; the work of the glycemia tests had to be interrupted because only the cages were marked, not the animals, and after the dispersion it was impossible to identify them.

Giulia came between one rabbit and the next, and told me point-blank that she needed me. I had come to the factory on my bike, right? Well, that very afternoon she had to go immediately all the way to Porta Genova, and to get there you had to take three different trams, she was in a hurry, it was an important business: would I please carry her on the crossbar, agreed? I, who according to the *commendatore*'s maniacal staggered schedule quit twelve minutes before she did, waited for her around the corner, settled her on the bike's crossbar, and we left.

Traveling around Milan on a bike was not at all daring in those days, and to carry a passenger on the crossbar at a time of bombings and with people leaving their homes to spend the night in a safer place was just about normal: sometimes, especially at night, it would happen that strangers would ask for this service, and for being transported from one end of the city to the other they would pay four or five lire. But Giulia, rather restless as a rule, that evening endangered our stability; she convulsively clutched the handlebar, making it hard to steer, suddenly changing her position with a jerk, illustrating her conversation with violent gestures of her hands and head, which shifted our common center of gravity in an unpredictable manner. Her conversation was at the start somewhat generic, but Giulia was not the type to bottle up her secrets and so harbor bile; halfway down Via Imbonati she had already left generalities behind, and at Porta Volta she spoke in quite explicit terms: she was furious because *his* parents had said no and she

*A rabbit in Italian is a *coniglio* and a tunnel is a *cunicolo*. Hence Levi's comment—TRANS.

was flying to the counterattack. Why had they said it?—for them I am not pretty enough, understand?—she snarled, shaking the handlebar.

"What idiots! You look pretty enough to me," I said seriously.

"Get smart. You don't know what it's all about."

"I only wanted to pay you a compliment; besides, that's what I think."

"This is not the moment. If you're trying to court me now, I'll knock you down."

"You'll fall, too."

"You're a fool. Go on, keep pedaling, it's getting late."

By the time we reached Largo Cairoli I already knew everything: or better, I possessed all the factual elements, but so confused and jumbled in their temporal sequence that it was not easy for me to make sense of them.

Above all, I could not understand how his will was not enough to overcome the problem—it was inconceivable, scandalous. There was this man, whom Giulia had at other times described to me as generous, solid, enamored, and serious; he possessed that girl, disheveled and splendid in her anger, who was writhing between my forearms intent on steering; and, instead of rushing to Milan to present his arguments, he was holed up in some border barracks to defend the nation. Because, being a *goy*, he was of course doing his military service: and as I was thinking like this and as Giulia continued to fight with me as if I were her Don Rodrigo,* I felt myself overcome by an absurd hatred for this never encountered rival. A *goy*, and she was a *goyá*, according to my atavistic terminology: and they could have gotten married. I felt growing within me, perhaps for the first time, a nauseating sensation of emptiness: so this is what it meant to be different: this was the price for being the salt of the earth. To carry on your crossbar a girl you desire and be so far from her as not to be able even to fall in love with her:

*A character in Manzoni's historical novel *The Betrothed*—TRANS.

carry her on your crossbar along Viale Gorizia to help her belong to someone else, and vanish from my life.

In front of No. 40 Viale Gorizia there was a bench: Giulia told me to wait for her there and flew through the street door like a gust of wind. I sat down and waited, battered and sorrowful. I thought that I ought to be less of a gentleman, indeed less inhibited and foolish, and that for the rest of my life I would regret that between myself and her there had been nothing but a few school and company memories; and that maybe it was not too late, that maybe the no of those two musical comedy parents would be adamant, that Giulia would come down in tears and I then could console her; and that these were infamous hopes, a wicked taking advantage of the misfortunes of others. And finally, the way a shipwrecked person tired of struggling lets himself sink straight to the bottom, I fell back on what was my dominant thought during those years: that the existing fiancé and the laws of racial separation were only stupid alibis, and that my inability to approach a woman was a condemnation without appeal which would accompany me to my death, confining me to a life poisoned by envy and by abstract, sterile, and aimless desires.

Giulia came out after two hours, in fact burst through the street door like a shell from a mortar. It was not necessary to question her to find out how things had gone: "I made them look *that* high," she said, all red in the face and still gasping. I made an effort to congratulate her in a believable fashion. But it's impossible to make Giulia believe things you don't really think, or hide things you do think. Now that she had thrown off that weight, and was shining with victory, she looked me straight in the eye, saw the shadow there, and asked, "What were you thinking about?"

"Phosphorus," I replied.

Giulia got married a few months later and said goodbye to me, snuffing tears up her nose and giving Varisco detailed alimentary instructions. She has had many hardships and many children; we *125* have remained friends, we see each other every so often in Milan and talk about chemistry and other reasonable matters. We are not dissatisfied with our choices and with what life has given us, but when we meet we both have a curious and not unpleasant impression (which we have both described to each other several times) that a veil, a breath, a throw of the dice deflected us onto two divergent paths, which were not ours.

G O L D

It is well known that people from Turin transplanted to Milan do not strike root, or at least do it badly. In the fall of 1942 there were seven of us friends from Turin, boys and girls, living in Milan, having arrived for different reasons in the large city which the war had rendered inhospitable; our parents—those of us who still had them—had moved to the country to avoid the bombings, and we were living an amply communal life. Euge was an architect, he wanted to do Milan over, and declared that the best city planner had been Frederick Barbarossa. Silvio had a law degree, but he was writing a philosophical treatise on minuscule sheets of onionskin and had a job with a shipping company. Ettore was an engineer at Olivetti's. Lina was sleeping with Euge and had some vague involvement with art galleries. *127*

Vanda was a chemist like me but could not find a job, and was permanently irritated by this because she was a feminist. Ada was my cousin and worked at the Corbaccio Publishing House; Silvio called her the bi-doctor because she had two degrees, and Euge called her *cousimo*, which meant cousin of Primo, which Ada rather resented. After Giulia's marriage, I had remained alone with my rabbits; I felt a widower and an orphan and fantasized about writing the saga of an atom of carbon, to make the people understand the solemn poetry, known only to chemists, of chlorophyll photosynthesis: and in fact I did eventually write it, but many years later, and it is the story with which this book concludes.

If I am not mistaken we were all writing poetry, except for Ettore, who said it was undignified for an engineer. Writing sad, crepuscular poems, and not all that beautiful, while the world was in flames, did not seem to us either strange or shameful: we proclaimed ourselves the enemies of Fascism, but actually Fascism had had its effect on us, as on almost all Italians, alienating us and making us superficial, passive, and cynical.

We bore with spiteful gaiety the rationing and the freezing cold in houses without coal, and we accepted with irresponsibility the nightly bombings by the English; they were not for us, they were a brutal sign of force on the part of our very distant allies, they didn't bother us. We thought what all humiliated Italians were then thinking: that the Germans and Japanese were invincible, but the Americans were too, and that the war would plod on like this for another twenty or thirty years, a bloody and interminable but remote stalemate, known only through doctored war bulletins, and sometimes, in certain of my contemporaries' families, through funereal, bureaucratic letters which spoke such words as "heroically, in the fulfillment of his duty." The *danse macabre* up and down the Libyan coast, back and forth on the steppes of the Ukraine, would never come to an end.

Each of us did his or her work day by day, slackly, without believing in it, as happens to someone who knows he is not working for his own future. We went to the theater and concerts, which sometimes were interrupted halfway through because the air-raid siren would start shrieking: and this seemed to us a ridiculous and gratifying incident; the Allies were masters of the sky, perhaps in the end they would win and Fascism would end—but it was their business, they were rich and powerful, they had the airplane carriers and the Liberators. But not us, "they" had declared us "different," and different we would be; we took sides but kept out of the stupid and cruel Aryan games, discussing the plays of O'Neill and Thornton Wilder, climbing the Grigne slopes, falling a bit in love with each other, inventing intellectual games, and singing the lovely songs Silvio had learned from some of his Waldensian friends. As to what was happening during those same months in all of Europe occupied by the Germans, in Ann Frank's house in Amsterdam, in the pit of Babi Yar near Kiev, in the ghetto of Warsaw, in Salonika, Paris, and Lidice: as to this pestilence which was about to submerge us no precise information had reached us, only vague and sinister hints dropped by soldiers returning from Greece or from the rear areas of the Russian front, and which we tended to censor. Our ignorance allowed us to live, as when you are in the mountains and your rope is frayed and about to break, but you don't know it and feel safe.

But in November came the Allied landing in North Africa, in December came the Russian resistance and finally victory at Stalingrad, and we realized that the war had drawn closer and that history had resumed its march. In the space of a few weeks each of us matured, more so than during the previous twenty years. Out of the shadows came men whom Fascism had not crushed—lawyers, professors, and workers—and we recognized in them our teachers, those for whom we had futilely searched until then in the Bible's doctrine, in chemistry, and on the mountains. Fascism had reduced them to silence for twenty years, and they explained to us that Fascism was not only a clownish and improvident misrule but the negator of justice; it had not only dragged Italy into an unjust and ill-omened war, but it had arisen and consolidated itself as the custodian of a detestable legality and order, based on the coercion of those who work, on the unchecked profits of those who exploit the labor of others, on the silence imposed on those who think and do not want to be slaves, and on systematic and calculated lies. They told us that our mocking, ironic intolerance was not enough; it should turn into anger, and the anger should be channeled into a well-organized and timely revolt, but they did not teach us how to make bombs or shoot a rifle.

They talked to us about unknowns: Gramsci, Salvemini, Gobetti, the Rosselli brothers—who were they? So there actually existed a second history, a history parallel to the one which the *liceo* had administered to us from on high? In those few convulsed months we tried in vain to reconstruct, repopulate the historic blank of the last twenty years, but those new characters remained "heroes," like Garibaldi and Nazario Sauro, they did not have thickness or human substance. The time to consolidate our education was not granted us: in March came the strikes in Turin, indicating that the crisis was near at hand: on July 25 came the internal collapse of Fascism, the piazzas jammed with happy, fraternal crowds, the spontaneous and precarious joy of a country to which liberty had been given by a palace intrigue; and then came the eighth of September, the gray-green serpent of Nazi divisions on the streets of Milan and Turin, the brutal reawakening: the comedy was over, Italy was an occupied country, like Poland, Yugoslavia, and Norway.

In this way, after the long intoxication with words, certain of the rightness of our choice, extremely insecure about our means, our hearts filled with much more desperation than hope, and against the backdrop of a defeated, divided country, we went into battle to test our strength. We separated to follow our destinies, each in a different valley.

We were cold and hungry, we were the most disarmed partisans in the Piedmont, and probably also the most unprepared. We
thought we were safe because we had not yet moved out of our

refuge buried under three feet of snow: but somebody betrayed us, and on the dawn of December 13, 1943, we woke surrounded by the Fascist Republic:* they were three hundred and we eleven, equipped with a tommy gun without bullets and a few pistols. Eight of us managed to escape and scattered among the mountains; three of us did not get away: the militiamen captured Aldo, Guido, and myself, still half asleep. As they came in I managed to hide in the stove's ashes the revolver I kept under my pillow, and which in any case I was not sure I knew how to use: it was tiny, all inlaid with mother of pearl, the kind used in movies by ladies desperately intent on committing suicide. Aldo, who was a doctor, stood up, stoically lit a cigarette, and said: "Too bad for my chromosomes."

They beat us up a bit, warned us "not to do anything ill-advised," promised to question us later in a certain very convincing manner of theirs and shoot us immediately afterward, ranged themselves with great pomp around us, and began walking us down toward the mountain pass. During the march, which lasted for several hours, I did two things that were very important to me: I ate bit by bit the much too false identity card I had in my wallet (the photograph was particularly disgusting), and, pretending to stumble, I slipped into the snow the notebook full of addresses I carried in my pocket. The militiamen were singing intrepid war songs, shooting at hares with their tommy guns, and flinging grenades into the streams to kill the trout. Down in the valley several buses were waiting for us. They made us get on and sit separately, and I had militiamen all around, seated and standing, who were not concerned about us and kept on singing. One of them, right in front of me, had his back to me and from his belt hung a hand grenade, one of those German hand grenades with a wooden handle. I could easily have lifted the safety pin, pulled the cord, and done away with myself and several of them, but I didn't have the courage. They

*This was the Republic of Saló, the puppet government set up by the Fascists in the north of Italy at Saló and under the protection of the Nazi army.

took us to the barracks, which were on the outskirts of Aosta. Their centurion was called Fossa, and it is strange, absurd, and sinisterly comic, given the situation at that time, that he lies now for decades in some out-of-the-way war cemetery and I am here, alive and substantially unharmed, writing this story. Fossa was a stickler for legality and set about rapidly organizing in our favor a prison regime which was in conformity with regulations. So he put us in the barracks' basement, one man per cell, with a cot and a pail, rations at eleven, an hour of open-air exercise, and the prohibition of talking to each other. This prohibition was painful because among us, in each of our minds, weighed an ugly secret: the same secret that had exposed us to capture, extinguishing in us, a few days before, all will to resist, indeed to live. We had been forced by our consciences to carry out a sentence and had carried it out, but we had come out of it destroyed, destitute, waiting for everything to finish and to be finished ourselves; but also wanting to see each other, to talk, to help each other exorcize that so recent memory. Now we were finished, and we knew it: we were in the trap, each one in his own trap, and there was no way out except down. It did not take me long to be convinced of it, examining my cell inch by inch, since the novels on which for years I had fed were full of miraculous escapes; but here the walls were half a yard thick, the door was massive and guarded on the outside, the small window was furnished with iron bars. I had a nail file, I could have sawn through one bar, perhaps even all of them; I was so thin that perhaps I could have squeezed through: but up against the window I discovered a large cement block to protect against bomb fragments during the air raids.

Every so often they came to get me for the interrogations. When Fossa was the interrogater, it wasn't too bad: Fossa was the sort of man I had never met until then—a Fascist by the book, stupid and courageous, whom the trade of soldiering (he had fought in Africa and Spain and boasted about it to us) had sheathed in solid ignorance and folly but had not corrupted nor made inhumane. He had believed and obeyed all of his life and was naively convinced that the persons guilty for the catastrophe were just two: the King and Galeazzo Ciano, who during those very days had been shot by a firing squad at Verona: not Badoglio, he too was a soldier, he had sworn loyalty to the King and he had kept faith with his oath. If it had not been for the King and Ciano, who had sabotaged the Fascist war from the start, everything would have gone well and Italy would have won. He regarded me as scatterbrained, spoiled by bad company; deep down in his class-oriented soul he was convinced that a man with a university degree could not really be "a subversive." He questioned me out of boredom, in order to indoctrinate me and give himself importance, but without any serious inquisitional intent: he was a soldier, not a cop. He never asked me embarrassing questions, nor did he ever ask me whether I was a Jew.

On the other hand, Cagni's interrogations were something to be afraid of. Cagni was the spy who had gotten us captured: a complete spy, in every ounce of his flesh, a spy by nature and tendency more than by Fascist conviction or for monetary gain; a spy to hurt, out of a kind of sporty sadism, as the hunter shoots free game. He was a skillful man: he had come with good credentials to a partisan formation next to ours, had passed himself off as the depository of important German military secrets, had revealed them, and later they proved artfully false and fabricated by the Gestapo. He organized the defense of the formation, put them through painstaking firefight exercises (in which he managed to get them to use up a good part of their ammunition), then fled to the valley and reappeared at the head of the Fascist platoons assigned to round up partisans. He was about thirty, with a pallid, flabby complexion; he began the interrogation by placing a Luger on his desk, prominently displayed, then hammered away for hours without a letup; he wanted to know everything. He continually threatened us with torture and the firing squad, but fortunately for me I knew almost nothing, and the few names I did know I kept to myself. He alternated moments of simulated cordiality with equally simulated explosions of rage; he told me (probably bluffing) that he knew I was a Jew, but that it was good for me: I was either a Jew or a partisan: if a partisan, he would put me against a wall; if a Jew, fine, there was a collection camp at Carpi, they were not bloody butchers, and I would remain there until the final victory. I admitted to being a Jew: partly because I was tired, partly out of an irrational digging in of pride, but I absolutely did not believe in his words. Had not he himself said that the control of that very barracks would within a few days be taken over by the SS?

In my cell there was a single dim bulb, which remained lit also at night; it was barely enough to read by, but all the same I read a great deal, because I thought the time left me was short. The fourth day, during the hour of open-air exercise, on the sly I put in my pocket a large stone because I wanted to try to communicate with Guido and Aldo, who were in adjoining cells. I succeeded, but it was exhausting: it took an hour to transmit a sentence, tapping it out in code on the wall between us, like the miners in *Germinal* buried in the mine. Pressing my ear against the wall to catch the reply, I heard instead the joyous, robust songs of the militiamen seated in the mess hall over our heads: *"the vision of . . . Aligheri"* or *"but I do not leave the tommy gun behind"* or, tearful among all of them, *"Come, there is a road in the woods."*

In my cell there was also a mouse. He kept me company, but at night he chewed my bread. There were two cots: I dismantled one of them and removed its long, smooth bar; I set it up vertically, and at night stuck the loaf of bread on its point, but would leave some of the crumbs on the floor for the mouse. I felt more like a mouse than he; I was thinking of the road in the woods, the snow outside, the indifferent mountains, the hundred splendid things which if I could go free I would be able to do, and a lump rose in my throat.

It was freezing. I knocked on the door until the militiaman came who was acting as a prison guard and asked him to let me see Fossa; the guard was actually the man who had beaten me when I was captured, but when he found out that I was a "doctor" he had begged my pardon: Italy is a strange country. He did not get me an interview, but he got blankets for me and the others and permission to warm up for a half hour every evening before lights-out by standing next to the boiler.

The new regime began that very evening. A militiaman came to get me, and he was not alone; with him was another prisoner whose existence I was unaware of. A pity: if it had been Guido or Aldo it would have been much better; however, he was a human being I could talk with. He took us to the boiler room, which was murky with soot, squeezed by a low ceiling, almost entirely encumbered by the boiler—but hot: a relief. The militiaman made us sit on a bench and took up a position himself on a chair in the door's opening, in order to obstruct it: he held his tommy gun upright between his knees, yet a few minutes later he was already dozing and had lost interest in us.

The prisoner looked at me with curiosity: "Are you the rebels?" he asked. He was perhaps thirty-five, was thin and a bit stooped, had kinky, unruly hair, a badly shaved beard, a large hooked nose, a lipless mouth, and shifty eyes. His hands were disproportionately large, gnarled, baked by sun and wind, and always moving: now he scratched himself, now he drummed on the bench or on his thigh; I noticed that they shook slightly. His breath smelled of wine, and from this I deduced that he had just been arrested; he had the accent of the valley thereabouts, but did not look like a peasant. I answered him, speaking in generalities, but he wasn't discouraged.

"He's asleep: you can talk if you want to. I can get news out of here: and anyway I may get out soon."

He didn't seem to me all that trustworthy. "Why are you here?" I asked.

"Contraband. I didn't want to share it with them, that's all. We'll end up coming to an agreement, but meanwhile they keep me here. It's bad, with my trade."

"It's bad for all trades!"

"But I have a special trade. I also do contraband, but only in the winter, when the Dora freezes over: so I do many different kinds of work, but none under a boss. We are free people: my father also was like this and my grandfather and all my great-grandfathers since the beginning of time, back to when the Romans came."

I had not understood the allusion to the frozen Dora and asked him to explain it: Was he a fisherman perhaps?

"You know why it's called the Dora?" he answered. "Because it's made of gold. Not all, of course, but it carries gold, and when it freezes over you can no longer take it out."

"Is there gold on the bottom?"

"Yes, in the sand: not everywhere, but in many stretches. It's the water that drags it down from the mountain and piles it up at random, there's some in one bend of the river and none in another. Our particular bend, which we have passed from father to son, is the richest of all: it is well hidden, very much out-of-the-way, but just the same it's best to go there at night so that nobody can come and poke around. Because of this, when it freezes over solid, as it did for instance last year, you can't work, because as soon as you've cut a hole in the ice more ice forms, and besides your hands can't stand it. If I were in your place and you in mine, on my word of honor, I'd even tell you where it is—our place."

I felt wounded by this sentence of his. I knew very well how things stood with me, but I didn't like to hear it said to me by a stranger. The other man, who realized his blunder, tried awkwardly to make amends:

"Well, what I meant to say is that these are confidential matters, which you don't even tell to your friends. I live on this, I have nothing else in this world, but I wouldn't change places with a banker. You see, it's not that there is so much gold: there is in fact very little, you wash it for a whole night and you manage to get two or three grams out of it: but it never ends. You can go back when you wish: the next night or a month later, whenever you feel like it, and the gold has grown back;

and it's that way forever and ever, like grass comes back in the fields. And so there are no people who are freer than us: that's why I feel I'm going crazy, staying inside here.

"Besides, you must understand that not everyone is able to wash sand, and that gives you satisfaction. My father taught me, just me, because I was the smartest; my other brothers work in the factory. And only to me he left the pan"—and with his enormous right hand slightly curled into a cup, he sketched the professional rotary movement.

"Not all days are good: it goes better when the weather is good and the moon in its last quarter. I couldn't say why, but that's how it is, in case it ever should occur to you to try."

I appreciated the good omen in silence. Of course I would try it: What wouldn't I try? During those days, when I was waiting courageously enough for death, I harbored a piercing desire for everything, for all imaginable human experiences, and I cursed my previous life, which it seemed to me I had profited from little or badly, and I felt time running through my fingers, escaping from my body minute by minute, like a hemorrhage that can no longer be stanched. Of course I would search for gold: not to get rich but to try out a new skill, to see again the earth, air, and water from which I was separated by a gulf that grew larger every day; and to find again my chemical trade in its essential and primordial form, the *Scheidekunst*, precisely, the art of separating metal from gangue.

"I don't sell it all," the man continued. "I am too fond of it. I keep a little on the side and melt it down, twice a year, and work it: I am not an artist but I like to have it in my hands, hit it with the hammer, score it, scratch it. I'm not interested in getting rich; what counts for me is to live free, not to have a collar like a dog, to work like this, when I wish, and nobody who can come and say, 'Come on, get moving.' That's why I hate staying in here; besides, on top of everything else, you lose a day's work."

The militiaman jerked in his sleep and the tommy gun that he held between his knees fell to the floor with a crash. The stranger and I exchanged a quick glance; we understood each other in a flash and rose with a jump from the bench: but we barely had time to take a step and already the militiaman had picked up his gun. He sat up, looked at his watch, cursed in Venetian dialect, and told us roughly that it was time to return to our cells. In the corridor we met Guido and Aldo, who, escorted by another guard, were on their way to take our place in the dusty fug of the boiler room: they greeted me with a nod of the head.

In the cell I was welcomed by the solitude, the freezing, pure breath of the mountains which came through the small window, and the anguish of tomorrow. I listened—in the silence of curfew one could hear the murmur of the Dora, lost friend, and all friends were lost, and youth and joy, and perhaps life: it flowed close by but indifferent, dragging along the gold in its womb of melted ice. I felt gripped by a painful envy for my ambiguous companion, who would soon return to his precarious but monstrously free life, to his inexhaustible trickle of gold, and an endless series of days.

CERIUM

The fact that I, a chemist, engaged here in writing my stories about chemistry, have lived a different season, has been narrated elsewhere.*

At a distance of thirty years I find it difficult to reconstruct the sort of human being that corresponded, in November 1944, to my name or, better, to my number: 174517. I must have by then overcome the most terrible crisis, the crisis of having become part of *Lager* system, and I must have developed a strange callousness if I then managed not only to survive but also to think, to register the world around me, and even to perform rather delicate work, in an environment infected by the

*My two books on Auschwitz: *If This Is a Man* and *The Truce* (Penguin Modern Classics, 1979).

daily presence of death and at the same time brought to a frenzy by the approach of the Russian liberators, who by now were only eighty kilometers away. Desperation and hope alternated at a rate that would have destroyed almost any normal person in an hour.

We were not normal because we were hungry. Our hunger at that time had nothing in common with the well-known (and not completely disagreeable) sensation of someone who has missed a meal and is certain that the next meal will not be missed: it was a need, a lack, a yearning that had accompanied us now for a year, had struck deep, permanent roots in us, lived in our cells, and conditioned our behavior. To eat, to get something to eat, was our prime stimulus, behind which, at a great distance, followed all the other problems of survival, and even still farther away the memories of home and the very fear of death.

I was a chemist in a chemical plant, in a chemical laboratory (this too has been narrated), and I stole in order to eat. If you do not begin as a child, learning how to steal is not easy; it had taken me several months before I could repress the moral commandments and acquired the necessary techniques, and at a certain point I realized (with a flash of laughter and a pinch of satisfied ambition) that I was reliving—*me*, a respectable little university graduate—the involution-evolution of a famous respectable dog, a Victorian, Darwinian dog who is deported and becomes a thief in order to live in his Klondike *Lager*—the great Buck of *The Call of the Wild*. I stole like him and like the foxes: at every favorable opportunity but with sly cunning and without exposing myself. I stole everything except the bread of my companions.

From the point of view, precisely, of substances that you could steal with profit, that laboratory was virgin territory, waiting to be explored. There was gasoline and alcohol, banal and inconvenient loot: many stole them, at various points in the plant, the offer was high and also the risk, since liquids require receptacles. This is the great problem of packaging, which every experienced chemist knows: and it was well known to God

Almighty, who solved it brilliantly, as he is wont to, with cellular membranes, eggshells, the multiple peel of oranges, and our own skins, because after all we too are liquids. Now, at that time, there did not exist polyethylene, which would have suited me perfectly since it is flexible, light, and splendidly impermeable: but it is also a bit too incorruptible, and not by chance God Almighty himself, although he is a master of polymerization, abstained from patenting it: He does not like incorruptible things.

Since I lacked the proper packaging materials, the ideal loot would therefore have had to be solid, not perishable, not cumbersome, and above all new. It had to be of high unitary value, that is, not voluminous, because we were often searched at the camp's entrance after work; and it should finally be useful to or desired by at least one of the social categories that composed the *Lager*'s complicated universe.

I had made various attempts in the lab. I had stolen a few hundred grams of fatty acids, laboriously obtained by the oxidation of paraffin from some colleagues of mine on the other side of the barrier: I had eaten half of it and it really took the edge off my hunger, but it had such a nasty taste that I gave up the idea of selling the remainder. I had tried to make fritters with sanitary cotton, which I pressed against an electric hot plate; they had a vague taste of burnt sugar, but they looked so awful that I did not consider them marketable. As for selling the cotton directly to the *Lager*'s infirmary, I had tried this once, but it was too cumbersome and not much sought after. I also forced myself to ingest and digest glycerin, basing myself on the simplistic reasoning that, since it is a product of the splitting of fats, it must after all in some way be metabolized and furnish calories: and perhaps it did furnish them, but at the cost of extremely unpleasant side effects.

There was a mysterious jar on one of the shelves. It contained about twenty gray, hard, colorless, tasteless little rods and did not have a label. This was very strange, because it was a German laboratory. Yes, of course, the Russians were a few kilometers away, catastrophe was in the air, almost visible; there were bombings every day; everybody knew the war was about to end: but finally some constants must still subsist, and among these were our hunger, that that laboratory was German, and that Germans never forget the labels. In fact, all the other jars and bottles in the lab had neat labels, written on the typewriter or by hand in beautiful Gothic characters—only that jar lacked a label.

In the situation I certainly did not dispose of the equipment and tranquility necessary to identify the nature of those small rods. Just to be sure, I hid three in my pocket and carried them with me that evening into the camp. They were about twenty-five millimeters long and had a diameter of four or five.

I showed them to my friend Alberto. Alberto took a penknife out of his pocket and tried to cut into one of them: it was hard, resisted the blade. He tried to scrape it: we heard a slight crepitation and saw a spray of yellow sparks. At this point diagnosis was easy: it was iron-cerium, an alloy from which the common flints of cigarette lighters are made. But why were they so large? Alberto, who for some weeks had worked as a laborer with a squad of welders, explained to me that they were mounted on the tips of oxyacetylene torches to ignite the flame. At this point I felt skeptical about the commercial possibilities of my stolen goods: they could perhaps be used to light a fire, but in the *Lager* matches (illegal) were certainly not scarce.

Alberto reproached me. For him renunciation, pessimism discouragement were abominable and culpable: he did not accept the concentration camp universe, he rejected it both instinctively and with his reason, and he did not let himself be tainted by it. He was a man of good and strong will, and miraculously he had remained free, and his words and his acts were free: he had not bowed his head, he had not bent his back. A gesture of his, a word, a smile had a liberating virtue, they were a rip in the rigid fabric of the *Lager*, and all those who had contact with him felt this, even those who did not understand his language. I believe that nobody, in that place, was loved as much as he was.

He reproached me: you should never be disheartened, because it is harmful and therefore immoral, almost indecent. I had stolen the cerium: good, now it's a matter of launching it. He would take care of it, he would turn it into a novelty, an article of high commercial value. Prometheus had been foolish to bestow fire on men instead of selling it to them: he would have made money, placated Jove, and avoided all that trouble with the vulture.

We must be more astute. This speech, about the necessity of being astute, was not new between us; Alberto had often made it to me, and before him others in the free world, and still many others repeated it to me later, an infinite number of times down to today, with a modest result; indeed, with the paradoxical result of developing in me a dangerous tendency of symbiosis with a truly astute person, who obtained (or felt he obtained) temporal or spiritual advantages from his companionship with me. Alberto was an ideal symbiont, because he refrained from being astute at my expense. I did not know, but he did (he always knew everything about everyone, and yet he didn't know German, or Polish, and had very little French), that in the plant there was a clandestine industry of cigarette lighters: unknown craftsmen, at spare moments, made them for important persons and civilian workers. Now flints are needed for lighters, and they had to be of a certain size: we had to thin down the rods I had. But how could we thin them down, and how much? "Don't make difficulties," he told me. "Leave it to me. You just worry about stealing the rest of them."

The next day I had no trouble in following Alberto's advice. Along about ten in the morning the siren of the *Fliegeralarm*—the air-raid alarm—burst out. It was nothing new by now, but each time this happened we felt—we and everyone—struck by anguish to the marrow of our bones. It did not seem an earthly sound, it was not a siren like those in the factories, it was a sound of enormous volume which, simultaneously and in cadence throughout the entire zone, rose to a spasmodic, acute note and redescended to a thunderous grumble. It could not have been a chance invention, since nothing in Germany took place by chance, and in any case it was too much in conformity with the goal and background: I have often thought that it had been elaborated by some malevolent musician, who locked in it fury and weeping, the wolf's howling at the moon and the breath of a typhoon: Astolfo's horn must have sounded like that. It provoked panic, not only because it announced the bombs to come but also because of its intrinsic horror, almost the lament of a wounded beast as all-encompassing as the horizon.

The Germans were more frightened than we were by the bombings: we, irrationally, did not fear them, because we knew that they were not aimed at us but at our enemies. In the space of a few seconds I found myself alone in the lab, pocketed all the cerium, and went out into the open to join my *Kommando*: the sky already resounded with the rumble of bombers, and from them fell, swaying softly, yellow leaflets which bore atrocious words of derision:

> *Im Bauch kein Fett,*
> *Acht Uhr ins Bett;*
> *Der Arsch kaum warm,*
> *Fliegeralarm!*

which, translated, ran:

> No lard in the gut
> At eight on the cot;
> Soon as the arse is warm
> Air-raid alarm!

We were not permitted to enter the air-raid shelters: we gathered in the vast areas not yet built up, around the rim of the plant. As the bombs began to fall, lying on the frozen mud and the sparse grass I felt the small rods in my pocket and meditated on the strangeness of my destiny, of our destinies as leaves on a branch, and on human destinies in general. According to Al-berto, the price of a lighter flint was equivalent to a ration of bread, that is, one day of life; I had stolen at least forty rods, from each of which could be obtained three finished flints. The total: one hundred and twenty flints, two months of life for me and two for Alberto, and in two months the Russians would have arrived and liberated us; and finally the cerium would have liberated us, an element about which I knew nothing, save for that single practical application, and that it belongs to the equivocal and heretical rare-earth group family, and that its name has nothing to do with the Latin and Italian word for wax (*cera*), and it was not named after its discoverer; instead it celebrates (great modesty of the chemists of past times!) the asteroid Ceres, since the metal and the star were discovered in the same year, 1801; and this was perhaps an affectionate-ironic homage to alchemical couplings: just as the Sun was gold and Mars iron, so Ceres must be cerium.

That evening I brought into camp the small rods and Alberto a metal plate with a round hole: it was the prescribed caliber to which we had to thin down the rods in order to transform them into flints and therefore bread.

What then occurred should be judged with caution. Alberto said that the rods must be reduced by scraping them with a knife, on the sly, so that no competitor could steal our secret. When? At night. Where? In the wooden hut, under the blankets and on top of the pallet full of shavings—thus running the risk of starting a fire and, more realistically, of being hanged: for this was the punishment meted out, among other transgressions, to all those who lit a match in the hut.

One always hesitates to judge foolhardy actions, whether one's own or those of others, after they have proven to be successful: perhaps therefore they were not foolhardy enough? Or perhaps it is true that there exists a God who protects children, fools, and drunks? Or perhaps again these actions have more weight and more warmth than those innumerable other actions that have ended badly, and one tells them more willingly? But we did not ask ourselves such questions: the *Lager* had given us a crazy familiarity with danger and death, and risking the noose to eat more seemed to us a logical, indeed an obvious choice.

While our companions slept, we worked with the knife, night after night. The scene was so sad you could weep: a single electric light bulb weakly lit the large wooden hut, and in the shadows, as in a vast cave, the faces of other men were visible, wracked by sleep and dreams: tinged with death, they worked their jaws furiously, dreaming of eating. Many of them had an arm or a naked, skeletal foot hanging over the side of the bunk, others moaned or talked in their sleep.

But we two were alive and did not give way to sleep. We kept the blanket raised with our knees and beneath that improvised tent scraped away at the small rods, blindly and by touch: at each stroke you heard a slight crackle and saw a spray of yellow sparks spurt up. At intervals we tested to see if the rod passed through the sample hole: if it didn't, we continued to scrape; if it did, we broke off the thinned-down stub and set it carefully aside.

We worked for three nights: nothing happened, nobody noticed our activity, nor did the blanket or pallet catch fire, and this is how we won the bread which kept us alive until the arrival of the Russians and how we comforted each other in the trust and friendship which united us. What happened to me is described elsewhere. Alberto left on foot with the majority of the prisoners when the front drew near: the Germans made them walk for days and nights in the snow and freezing cold, slaughtering all those who could not go on: then they loaded them on open freight cars, which transported the few survivors to a new chapter of slavery, Buchenwald and Mauthausen. Nor more than a fourth of those who left survived the march.

Alberto did not return, and not a trace remains of him; after the end of the war a man from his town, half visionary and half crook, lived for a number of years on the money he made telling his mother false consolatory tales about him.

CHROMIUM

The entrée was fish, but the wine was red. Versino, head of maintenance, said that it was all a lot of nonsense, provided the wine and fish were good; he was certain that the majority of those who upheld the orthodox view could not, blindfolded, have distinguished a glass of white wine from a glass of red. Bruni, from the Nitro Department, asked whether somebody knew why fish goes with white wine: various joking remarks were made but nobody was able to answer properly. Old man Cometto added that life is full of customs whose roots can no longer be traced: the color of sugar paper, the buttoning from different sides for men and women, the shape of a gondola's prow, and the innumerable alimentary compatibilities and incompatibilities, of which in fact the one in question was a particular case: but in any event, why were pig's feet obligatory with lentils, and cheese on macaroni.

I made a rapid mental review to be sure that none of those present had as yet heard it, then I started to tell the story of the onion in the boiled linseed oil. This, in fact, was a dining room for a company of varnish manufacturers, and it is well known that boiled linseed oil has for many centuries constituted the fundamental raw material of our art. It is an ancient art and therefore noble: its most remote testimony is in Genesis 6:14, where it is told how, in conformity with a precise specification of the Almighty, Noah coated (probably with a brush) the Ark's interior and exterior with melted pitch. But it is also a subtly fraudulent art, like that which aims at concealing the substratum by conferring on it the color and appearance of what it is not: from this point of view it is related to cosmetics and adornment, which are equally ambiguous and almost equally ancient arts (Isaiah 3:16). Given therefore its pluri-millenial origins, it is not so strange that the trade of manufacturing varnishes retains in its crannies (despite the innumerable solicitations it modernly receives from kindred techniques) rudiments of customs and procedures abandoned for a long time now.

So, returning to boiled linseed oil, I told my companions at table that in a prescription book published about 1942 I had found the advice to introduce into the oil, toward the end of the boiling, two slices of onion, without any comment on the purpose of this curious additive. I had spoken about it in 1949 with Signor Giacomasso Olindo, my predecessor and teacher, who was then more than seventy and had been making varnishes for fifty years, and he, smiling benevolently behind his thick white mustache, had explained to me that in actual fact, when he was young and boiled the oil personally, thermometers had not yet come into use: one judged the temperature of the batch by observing the smoke, or spitting into it, or, more efficiently, immersing a slice of onion in the oil on the point of a skewer; when the onion began to fry, the boiling was finished. Evidently, with the passing of the years, what had been a crude measuring operation had lost its significance and was transformed into a mysterious and magical practice.

Old Cometto told of an analogous episode. Not without nostalgia he recalled his good old times, the times of copal gum: he told how once boiled linseed oil was combined with these legendary resins to make fabulously durable and gleaming varnishes. Their fame and name survive now only in the locution "copal shoes," which alludes precisely to a varnish for leather at one time very widespread that has been out of fashion for at least the last half century. Today the locution itself is almost extinct. Copals were imported by the British from the most distant and savage countries, and bore their names, which in fact distinguished one kind from another: copal of Madagascar or Sierra Leone or Kauri (whose deposits, let it be said parenthetically, were exhausted along about 1967), and the very well known and noble Congo copal. They are fossil resins of vegetable origin, with a rather high melting point, and in the state in which they are found and sold in commerce are insoluble in oil: to render them soluble and compatible they were subjected to a violent, semi-destructive boiling, in the course of which their acidity diminished (they decarboxylated) and also the melting point was lowered. The operation was carried out in a semi-industrial manner by direct fire in modest, mobile kettles of four or six hundred pounds; during the boiling they were weighed at intervals, and when the resin had lost 16 percent of its weight in smoke, water vapor, and carbon dioxide, the solubility in oil was judged to have been reached. Along about 1940, the archaic copals, expensive and difficult to supply during the war, were supplanted by phenolic and maleic resins, both suitably modified, which, besides costing less, were directly compatible with the oils. Very well: Cometto told us how, in a factory whose name shall not be uttered, until 1953 a phenolic resin, which took the place of the Congo copal in a formula, was treated exactly like copal itself—that is, by consuming 16 percent of it on the fire, amid pestilential phenolic exhalations—until it had reached that solubility in oil which the resin already possessed. *149*

Here at this point I remembered that all languages are full of images and metaphors whose origin is being lost, together with the art from which they were drawn: horsemanship having declined to the level of an expensive sport, such expressions as "belly to the ground" and "taking the bit in one's teeth" are unintelligible and sound odd; since mills with superimposed stones have disappeared, which were also called millstones, and in which for centuries wheat (and varnishes) were ground, such a phrase as "to eat like four millstones" sounds odd and even mysterious today. In the same way, since Nature too is conservative, we carry in our coccyx what remains of a vanished tail.

Bruni told us about an episode in which he himself had been involved, and as he told the story, I felt myself invaded by sweet and tenuous sensations which later I will try to explain. I must say first of all that Bruni worked from 1955 to 1965 in a large factory on the shores of a lake, the same one in which I had learned the rudiments of the varnish-making trade during the years 1946–47. So he told us that, when he was down there in charge of the Synthetic Varnishes Department, there fell into his hands a formula of a chromate-based anti-rust paint that contained an absurd component: nothing less than ammonium chloride, the old, alchemical sal ammoniac of the temple of Ammon, much more apt to corrode iron than preserve it from rust. He had asked his superiors and the veterans in the department about it: surprised and a bit shocked, they had replied that in that formulation, which corresponded to at least twenty or thirty tons of the product a month and had been in force for at least ten years, that salt "had always been in it," and that he had his nerve, so young in years and new on the job, criticizing the factory's experience, and looking for trouble by asking silly hows and whys. If ammonium chloride was in the formula, it was evident that it had some sort of use. What use it had nobody any longer knew, but one should be very careful about taking it out because "one never knows." Bruni is a rationalist, and he took all this very badly; but he is a prudent man, and so he accepted the advice, according to which in that formulation and in that lakeshore factory, unless there have been further developments, ammonium chloride is still being put in; and yet today it is completely useless, as I can state from firsthand experience because it was I who introduced it into the formula.

The episode cited by Bruni, the rustproof formula with chromates and ammonium chloride, flung me back in time, all the way to the freezing cold January of 1946, when meat and coal were still rationed, nobody had a car, and never in Italy had people breathed so much hope and so much freedom.

But I had returned from captivity three months before and was living badly. The things I had seen and suffered were burning inside of me; I felt closer to the dead than the living, and felt guilty at being a man, because men had built Auschwitz, and Auschwitz had gulped down millions of human beings, and many of my friends, and a woman who was dear to my heart. It seemed to me that I would be purified if I told its story, and I felt like Coleridge's Ancient Mariner, who waylays on the street the wedding guests going to the feast, inflicting on them the story of his misfortune. I was writing concise and bloody poems, telling the story at breakneck speed, either by talking to people or by writing it down, so much so that gradually a book was later born: by writing I found peace for a while and felt myself become a man again, a person like everyone else, neither a martyr nor debased nor a saint: one of those people who form a family and look to the future rather than the past.

Since one can't live on poetry and stories, I looked feverishly for work and found it in the big lakeshore factory, still damaged from the war, and during those months besieged by mud and ice. Nobody was much concerned with me: colleagues, the director, and workers had other things to think about—the son who wasn't returning from Russia, the stove without wood, the shoes without soles, the warehouses without supplies, the windows without panes, the freezing cold which split the pipes, inflation, famine, and the virulent local feuds. I had been benignly granted a lame-legged desk in the lab, in a corner full   *151* of crashing noise, drafts, and people coming and going carrying rags and large cans, and I had not been assigned a specific task. I, unoccupied as a chemist and in a state of utter alienation (but then it wasn't called that), was writing in a haphazard fashion page after page of the memories which were poisoning me, and my colleagues watched me stealthily as a harmless nut. The book grew under my hands, almost spontaneously, without plan or system, as intricate and crowded as an anthill. Every so often, impelled by a feeling of professional conscience, I would ask to see the director and request some work, but he was much too busy to worry about my scruples. I should read and study; when it came to paints and varnishes I was still, if I didn't mind his saying so, an illiterate. I didn't have anything to do? Well, I should praise God and sit in the library; if I really had the itch to do something useful, well, look, there were articles to translate from German.

One day he sent for me and with an oblique glint in his eyes announced that he had a little job for me. He took me to a corner of the factory's yard, near a retaining wall: piled up at random, the lowest crushed by the highest, were thousands of square blocks of a bright orange color. He told me to touch them: they were gelatinous and softish; they had the disagreeable consistency of slaughtered tripes. I told the director that, apart from the color, they seemed to me to be livers, and he praised me: that's just how it was described in the paint manuals! He explained that the phenomenon which had produced them was called just that in English, "livering"; under certain conditions certain paints turned from liquids into solids, with the consistency precisely of the liver or lungs, and must be thrown out. These parallelepiped shapes had been cans of paint: the paint had livered, the cans had been cut away, and the contents had been thrown on the garbage dump.

That paint, he told me, had been produced during the war and immediately after; it contained a basic chromate and alkyd resin. Perhaps the chromate was too basic or the resin too acidic: these were exactly the conditions under which a "livering" can take place. All right, he made me the gift of that pile of old sins; I should think about it, make tests and examinations, and try to say with precision why the trouble had occurred, what should be done so that it was not repeated, and if it were possible to reclaim the damaged goods.

Thus set forth, half chemistry and half police work, the problem attracted me: I was reconsidering it that evening (it was Saturday evening) as one of the sooty, freezing freight trains of that period lugged me to Turin. Now it happened that the next day destiny reserved for me a different and unique gift: the encounter with a woman, young and made of flesh and blood, warm against my side through our overcoats, gay in the humid mist of the avenues, patient, wise and sure as we were walking down streets still bordered with ruins. In a few hours we knew that we belonged to each other, not for one meeting but for life, as in fact has been the case. In a few hours I felt reborn and replete with new powers, washed clean and cured of a long sickness, finally ready to enter life with joy and vigor; equally cured was suddenly the world around me, and exorcized the name and face of the woman who had gone down into the lower depths with me and had not returned. My very writing became a different adventure, no longer the dolorous itinerary of a convalescent, no longer a begging for compassion and friendly faces, but a lucid building, which now was no longer solitary: the work of a chemist who weighs and divides, measures and judges on the basis of assured proofs, and strives to answer questions. Alongside the liberating relief of the veteran who tells his story, I now felt in the writing a complex, intense, and new pleasure, similar to that I felt as a student when penetrating the solemn order of differential calculus. It was exalting to search and find, or create, the right word, that is, commensurate, concise, and strong; to dredge up events from my memory and describe them with the greatest rigor and the least clutter. Paradoxically, my baggage of atrocious memories became a wealth, a seed; it seemed to me that, by writing, I was growing like a plant.

In the freight train of the following Monday, squeezed in a sleepy crowd bundled in scarfs, I felt full of joy and alert as never before or after. I was ready to challenge everything and everyone, in the same way that I had challenged and defeated Auschwitz and loneliness: disposed, especially, to engage in joyous battle with the clumsy pyramid of orange livers that awaited me on the lakeshore.

It is the spirit that dominates matter, is that not so? Was it not this that they had hammered into my head in the Fascist and Gentile *liceo*? I threw myself into the work with the same intensity that, at not so distant a period, we had attacked a rock wall; and the adversary was still the same, the not-I, the Button Molder,* the *hyle*: stupid matter, slothfully hostile as human stupidity is hostile, and like it strong because of its obtuse passivity. Our trade is to conduct and win this interminable battle: a livered paint is much more rebellious, more refractory to your will than a lion in its mad pounce; but, let's admit it, it's also less dangerous.

The first skirmish took place in the archives. The two partners, the two fornicators from whose embrace had sprung our orange-colored monsters, were the chromate and the resin. The resin was fabricated on the spot: I found the birth certificate of all the batches, and they did not offer anything suspicious; the acidity was variable, but always inferior to 6, as prescribed. One batch that was found to have a pH of 6.2 had been dutifully discarded by an inspector with a flowery signature. In the first instance the resin could not be faulted.

The chromate had been purchased from different suppliers, and it too had been duly inspected batch by batch. According to Purchase Specification 480/0 it should have contained not less than 28 percent of chromium oxide in all; and now here, right before my eyes I had the interminable list of tests from January 1942 until today (one of the least exciting forms of reading imaginable), and all the values satisfied the specification, indeed

154   *A character in Ibsen's* Peer Gynt.

were equal among themselves: 29.5 percent, not one percent more, not one less. I felt my inner being as a chemist writhe, confronted by that abomination; in fact, one should know that the natural oscillations in the method of preparation of such a chromate, added to the inevitable analytical errors, make it extremely improbable that the many values found in different batches and on different days could coincide so exactly. How come nobody had gotten suspicious? But in fact at that time I did not yet know the frightening anesthetic power of company papers, their capacity to hobble, douse, and dull every leap of intuition and every spark of talent. It is well known to the scholarly that all secretions can be harmful or toxic: now under pathological conditions it is not rare that the paper, a company secretion, is reabsorbed to an excessive degree, and puts to sleep, paralyzes, or actually kills the organism from which it has been exuded.

The story of what had happened began to take shape. For some reason, some analyst had been betrayed by a defective method, or an impure reagent, or an incorrect habit; he had diligently totted up those so obviously suspicious but formally blameless results; he had punctiliously signed each analysis, and his signature, swelling like an avalanche, had been consolidated by the signatures of the lab chief, the technical director, and the general director. I could see him, the poor wretch, against the background of those difficult years: no longer young, since all the young men were in the military services; perhaps chivied by the Fascists, perhaps himself a Fascist being looked for by the partisans; certainly frustrated, because being an analyst is a young man's job; on guard in his lab within the fortress of his minuscule specialty, since the analyst is by definition infallible; and derided and regarded with a hostile eye outside the lab just because of his virtues as an incorruptible guardian, a severe, pedantic, unimaginative little judge, a stick poked in the wheels of production. To judge from the anonymous, neat handwriting, his trade must have exhausted him and at the same time brought him to a crude perfection, like a pebble in a mountain stream that has been twirled over and over all the way to the stream's mouth. It was not surprising that, with time, he had developed a certain insensitivity to the real significance of the operations he was performing and the notes he was writing. I planned to look into his particular case but nobody knew anything more about him; my questions were met with discourteous or absentminded replies. Moreover, I was beginning to feel around me and my work a mocking and malevolent curiosity: who was this Johnny-come-lately, this pipsqueak earning 7,000 lire a month, this maniac scribbler who was disturbing the nights of the guest quarters typing away at God knows what, and sticking his nose into past mistakes and washing a generation's dirty linen? I even had the suspicion that the job that had been assigned me had the secret purpose of getting me to bump into something or somebody; but by now this matter of the livering absorbed me body and soul, *tripes et boyaux*—in short, I was enamored of it almost as of that aforementioned girl, who in fact was a little jealous of it.

It was not hard for me to procure, besides the Purchase Specification (the PS), also the equally inviolable CS, the Checking Specifications: in a drawer in the lab there was a packet of greasy file cards, typewritten and corrected several times by hand, each of which contained the way to carry out a check of a specific raw material. The file card on prussian blue was stained with blue, the file card on glycerine was sticky, and the file card on fish oil smelled like sardines. I took out the file card on chromate, which due to long use had become the color of a sunrise, and read it carefully. It was all rather sensible and in keeping with my not-so-far-off scholastic notions; only one point seemed strange to me. Having achieved the disintegration of the pigment, it prescribed adding twenty-three drops of a certain reagent. Now, a drop is not so definite a unit as to entail so definite a numerical coefficient; and besides, when all is said and done, the prescribed dose was absurdly high: it would have flooded the analysis, leading in any case to a result in keeping with the specification. I looked at the back of the file card: it bore the date of the last review, January 4, 1944; the birth certificate of the first livered batch was on the succeeding February 22.

At this point I began to see the light. In a dusty archive I found the CS collection no longer in use, and there, lo and behold, the preceding edition of the chromate file card bore the direction to add "2 or 3" drops, and not "23": the fundamental "or" was half erased and in the next transcription had gotten lost. The events meshed perfectly: the revision of the file card had caused a mistake in transcription, and the mistake had falsified all succeeding analyses, concealing the results on the basis of a fictitious value due to the reagent's enormous excess and thus bringing about the acceptance of shipments of pigment which should have been discarded; these, being too basic, had brought about the livering.

But there is trouble in store for anyone who surrenders to the temptation of mistaking an elegant hypothesis for a certainty: the readers of detective stories know this quite well. I got hold of the sleepy man in charge of the storeroom, requested from him all the samples of all the shipments of chromate from January 1944 on, and barricaded myself behind a workbench for three days in order to analyze them according to the incorrect and correct methods. Gradually, as the results lined up in a column on the register, the boredom of repetitious work was being transformed into nervous gaiety, as when as children you play hide and seek and discover your opponent clumsily squatting behind a hedge. With the mistaken method you constantly found the fateful 29.5 percent; with the correct method, the results were widely dispersed, and a good quarter, being inferior to the prescribed minimum, corresponded to the shipments which should have been rejected. The diagnosis was confirmed, the pathogenesis discovered: it was now a matter of defining the therapy.

This was found pretty soon, drawing on good inorganic chemistry, that distant Cartesian island, a lost paradise, for us organic chemists, bunglers, "students of gunks": it was necessary to neutralize in some way, within the sick body of that varnish, the excess of basicity due to free lead oxide. The acids were shown to be noxious from other aspects: I thought of ammonium chloride, capable of combining stably with lead oxide, producing an insoluble and inert chloride and freeing the ammonia. Tests on a small scale gave promising results: now quick, find the chloride, come to an agreement with the head of the Milling Department, slip into a small ball mill two of the livers disgusting to see and touch, add a weighed quantity of the presumed medicine, start the mill under the skeptical eyes of the onlookers. The mill, usually so noisy, started almost grudgingly, in a silence of bad omen, impeded by the gelatinous mass which stuck to the balls. All that was left was to go back to Turin to wait for Monday, telling the patient girl in whirlwind style the hypotheses arrived at, the things understood at the lakeshore, the spasmodic waiting for the sentence that the facts would pronounce.

The following Monday the mill had regained its voice: it was in fact crunching away gaily with a full, continuous tone, without that rhythmic roaring that in a ball mill indicates bad maintenance or bad health. I stopped it and cautiously loosened the bolts on the manhole; there spurted out with a hiss an ammoniacal puff, as it should. Then I took off the cover. Angels and ministers of grace!—the paint was fluid and smooth, completely normal, born again from its ashes like the Phoenix. I wrote out a report in good company jargon and the management increased my salary. Besides, as a form of recognition, I received the assignment of two tires for my bike.

Since the storeroom contained several shipments of perilously basic chromate, which must also be utilized because they had been accepted by the inspection and could not be returned to the supplier, the chloride was officially introduced as an anti-livering preventive in the formula of that varnish. Then I quit my job: ten years went by, the postwar years were over, the deleterious, too basic chromates disappeared from the market, and my report went the way of all flesh: but formulas are as holy as prayers, decree-laws, and dead languages, and not an iota in them can be changed. And so my ammonium chloride, the twin of a happy love and a liberating book, by now completely useless and probably a bit harmful, is religiously ground into the chromate anti-rust paint on the shore of that lake, and nobody knows why anymore.

SULFUR

Lanza hooked the bike to the rack, punched the time card, went
to the boiler, put the mixer in gear, and started the motor. The
jet of pulverized naphtha ignited with a violent thud, and a
perfidious backfire shot out (but Lanza, knowing that furnace,
had gotten out of the way in time): then it continued to burn
with a good, taut, full roar, like continuous thunder, which
covered the low hum of the motors and transmissions. Lanza
was still heavy with the sleep and cold of a sudden awakening;
he remained squatting in front of the furnace, whose red blaze,
in a succession of rapid gleams, made his enormous, crazed
shadow dance on the back wall, as in some primitive movie
house.

After half an hour the thermometer began to move, as it

should: the hand of burnished steel, slithering like a snail over the dark yellow face, came to a stop at 95 degrees. This too was right, because the thermometer was off by five degrees; Lanza was satisfied and obscurely at peace with the boiler, the thermometer, and, in short, the world and himself because all the things which should happen were happening, and because in the factory he alone knew that the thermometer was off: perhaps another man would have given a boost to the fire, or would have started to figure out who knows what to make it rise to 100 degrees, as it was written on the worksheet.

So the thermometer halted for a long time at 95 degrees and then began to climb again. Lanza remained close to the fire, and since, with the warmth, sleep began pressing in on him again, he permitted it softly to invade some of the rooms of his consciousness. But not that which stood behind his eyes and watched the thermometer: that must remain wide awake.

With a sulfodiene one never knows, but for the moment everything was going properly. Lanza enjoyed the quiet rest, going along with the dance of thoughts and images that is the prelude to sleep, yet avoiding being overcome by it. It was hot, and Lanza saw his hometown—his wife, his son, his field, the tavern. The warm breath of the tavern, the heavy breath of the stable. Water trickled into the stable with every rainstorm, water that came from above, from the hayloft—perhaps from a crack in the wall, because all the roof tiles (he had checked them himself at Easter) were in perfect condition. There is room for another cow, but (here everything became fogged over by a mist of sketchy and unfinished calculations). Every minute of work put ten lire into his pocket: now he felt as if the fire was roaring for him, that the mixer was turning for him, like a machine to make money.

On your feet, Lanza, we have arrived at 180 degrees, we've got to unbolt the kettle hatch and throw in the B 41: but to go on calling it B 41 is really a big joke when the whole factory knows that it is sulfur, and in time of war, when everything was lacking, many took it home and sold it on the black market to the peasants who dust the vines with it. But if that's how the boss wants it, that's what he gets.

He switched off the fire, slowed up the mixer, unbolted the hatch, and put on the protective mask, which made him feel like half a mole and half a wild boar. The B 41 was already weighed out, in three cardboard boxes: he put it in cautiously and, despite the mask, which may have leaked a bit, immediately smelled the dirty, sad smell that emanated from the mixture, and thought that maybe the priest was right too, when he said that in Hell there is a smell of sulfur: after all, even the dogs don't like it, everyone knows that. When he was finished, he shut the door and started everything up again.

At three in the morning the thermometer stood at 200 degrees: it was time for the vacuum. He lifted the black lever and the high, sharp racket of the centrifugal pump was superimposed on the deep thunder of the burner. The needle of the vacuum gauge, which stood vertical at zero, began to fall, sliding to the left. Twenty degrees, forty degrees: good. At this point you can light a cigarette and take it easy for more than an hour.

Some are fated to become millionaires, and some are fated to drop dead. He, Lanza, was fated (and he yawned noisily to keep himself company) to make night into day. As if they too had guessed it, during the war they had immediately shoved him into the great job of staying up nights on the rooftops to shoot planes out of the sky.

With a jump he was on his feet, his ears listening tensely and all his nerves in alarm. The clatter of the pump had suddenly become slower and more clogged, as though constrained: and in fact, the needle of the vacuum gauge, like a threatening finger, rose up to zero, and, look! degree by degree, it began to slide to the right. That was it, the kettle was building up pressure.

"Turn it off and run." "Turn everything off and run." But he did not run: he grabbed a wrench and banged the vacuum pipe along its entire length: it had to be obstructed, there could be no other reason. Bang again and bang again: nothing, the pump continued to grind away, and the needle bounced around at about a third of an atmosphere.

Lanza felt all his hairs standing on end, like the tail of an enraged cat: and he was enraged, in a murderous, wild rage against the kettle, against that ugly, reluctant beast crouched on the fire, which lowed like a bull: red hot, like an enormous hedgehog with its quills standing straight up, so that you do not know where to touch and seize it and you feel like jumping on it and kicking it to pieces. His fists clenched and his head bursting, Lanza was in a frenzy to open the hatch and let the pressure escape; he began to loosen the bolts, and, look! a yellowish slime squirted hissing from the crack together with puffs of foul smoke: the kettle must be full of foam. Lanza slammed it shut, filled with an overwhelming desire to get on the phone and call the boss, call the fireman, call the Holy Ghost to come out of the night and give him a hand or at least advice.

The kettle was not built for pressure and could explode from one moment to the next; or at least that's what Lanza thought, and perhaps, if it had been during the day or he hadn't been alone, he would not have thought that. But his fear had turned into anger, and when his anger had simmered down it left his head cold and uncluttered. And then he thought of the most obvious thing: he opened the valve of the suction fan, started it going, closed the vacuum breaker, and stopped the pump. With relief and pride because he had correctly figured it out, he saw the needle rise up all the way to zero, like a stray sheep that returns to the fold, and then slide gently down on the vacuum side.

He looked around, with a great need to laugh and tell it to somebody and with a feeling of lightness in all his limbs. He saw on the floor his cigarette reduced to a long thin cylinder of ash: it had smoked itself. It was five twenty, dawn was breaking behind the shed of empty barrels, the thermometer pointed to 210 degrees. He took a sample from the boiler, let it cool, and tested it with the reagent: the test tube remained clear for a few seconds and then became white as milk. Lanza turned off the fire, stopped the mixer and the fan, and opened the vacuum breaker: he heard a long, angry hiss, which gradually calmed down into a rustle, a murmur, and then fell silent. He screwed in the siphon pipe, started the compressor, and, gloriously, surrounded by white puffs of smoke and the customary sharp smell, the dense jet of resin came to rest in the collection basin, forming a black shiny mirror.

Lanza went to the main gate and met Carmine, who was coming in. He told him that everything was going well, left him the work orders, and began pumping up his bike's tires.

TITANIUM

To Felice Fantino

In the kitchen there was a very tall man dressed in a way Maria had never seen before. On his head he wore a boat made out of a newspaper, he smoked a pipe, and he was painting the closet white.

It was incomprehensible how all that white could be contained in so small a can, and Maria had a great desire to go over and look inside it. Every so often the man rested his pipe on the closet and whistled; then he stopped whistling and began to sing; every so often he took two steps back and closed one eye, and also at times he would go and spit in the garbage can, then he rubbed his mouth with the back of his hand. In short he did so many strange and new things that it was very interesting to stay there and watch him: and when the closet was white, he picked up the pot and many newspapers that were on the floor and carried everything next to the cupboard and began to paint that too.

The closet was so shiny, clean, and white that it was almost indispensable to touch it. Maria went up to the closet, but the man noticed and said, "Don't touch. You mustn't touch."

Maria stopped in amazement and asked, "Why?" to which the man replied, "Because you shouldn't." Maria thought about that, and then asked again, "Why is it so white?" The man also thought for a while, as if the question seemed difficult to him, and then said in a deep voice, "Because it is titanium."*

Maria felt a delicious shiver of fear run through her, as when in the fairy tale you get to the ogre; so she looked carefully and saw that the man did not have knives either in his hand or near him: but he could have one hidden. Then she asked, "Cut what on me?"—and at this point he should have replied, "Cut your tongue." Instead, he only said, "I'm not cutting anything: this is titanium."

In conclusion, he must be a very powerful man: but he did not seem to be angry, but rather good-natured and friendly. Maria asked him, "Mister, what's your name?" He replied, "Felice." He had not taken his pipe out of his mouth, and when he spoke his pipe danced up and down but did not fall. Maria stood there for a while in silence, looking alternately at the man and the closet. She was not at all satisfied by that answer and would have liked to ask him why he was named Felice, but then she did not dare, because she remembered that children must never ask why. Her friend Alice was called Alice and was a child,

*There are two untranslatable plays on words on this page. When the man says "titanium" Maria hears the Italian words *Ti taglio* due to the slurring caused by his pipe; the words mean "I cut you." When she muses over the similarity of Alice and Felice, it is because small anchovies are called *alice* and because the two names have a similarity to this and each other due to their Italian pronunciation, thus *ahh-lee-chay*, *fay-lee-chay*—TRANS.

and it was really strange that a big man like that should be called Felice. But little by little, however, it began to seem natural to her that the man should be called Felice, and in fact she thought he could not have been called anything else.

The painted closet was so white that in comparison all the rest of the kitchen looked yellow and dirty. Maria decided there was nothing wrong in going to look at it up close, only look, without touching. But as she was approaching on tiptoe an unexpected and terrible thing happened: the man turned, and in two steps was beside her; he took out of his pocket a white chalk and drew a circle on the floor around Maria. Then he said, "You must stay in there." After which he struck a match, lit his pipe, making many strange grimaces with his mouth, and resumed painting the cupboard.

Maria sat on her heels and considered the circle for a long time and attentively: but she became convinced that there was no way out. She tried to rub it at one spot with her finger and saw that the chalk line actually disappeared; but she understood very well that the man would not have regarded that system as valid.

The circle was evidently magical. Maria sat on the floor silent and quiet; every so often she tried to reach far enough to touch the circle with the tips of her feet and leaned forward so far that she almost lost her balance, but she soon realized that there still was a good hand's breadth before she could reach the closet or wall with her fingers. So she just sat there and watched as gradually the cupboard, chairs, and table also became white and beautiful.

After a very long time the man put down his brush and paint pot and took the newspaper boat off his head, and then you could see that he had hair like all other men. Then he went out by the balcony and Maria heard him rummaging around and tramping up and down in the next room. Maria began to call, "Mister!"—first in a low voice, then louder, but not too loud because at bottom she was afraid that the man might hear.

Finally the man returned to the kitchen. Maria asked, "Mister, can I come out now?" The man looked down at Maria in the circle, laughed loudly, and said many things that were incomprehensible, but he didn't seem angry. At last he said, "Yes, of course, now you can come out." Maria looked at him perplexed and did not move; then the man picked up a rag and wiped away the circle very carefully, to undo the enchantment. When the circle had disappeared, Maria got up and left, skipping, and she felt very happy and satisfied.

A R S E N I C

He had an unusual appearance for a customer. To our humble and enterprising laboratory, hiring us to analyze the most disparate materials, came all sorts of people, men and women, old and young, but all visibly members of the large, ambiguous, and cunning network of commerce. Anyone who has the trade of buying and selling is easily recognized: he has a vigilant eye and a tense face, he fears fraud or considers it, and he is on guard like a cat at dusk. It is a trade that tends to destroy the immortal soul; there have been courtier philosophers, lens-grinding philosophers, and even engineer and strategist philosophers; but no philosopher, so far as I know, was a wholesaler or storekeeper.

I received him, since Emilio was not there. He could have been a peasant philosopher: he was a robust and rubicund old man, with heavy hands deformed by work and arthritis; his eyes looked clear, mobile, youthful, despite the large delicate bags that hung slackly under his eye sockets. He wore a vest, from whose small pocket dangled a watch chain. He spoke Piedmontese, which immediately made me ill at ease: it is not good manners to reply in Italian to someone who speaks in dialect, it puts you immediately on the other side of a barrier, on the side of the aristos, the respectable folk, the "Luigini," as they were called by my illustrious namesake;* but my Piedmontese, correct in form and sound, is so smooth and enervated, so polite and languid, that it does not seem very authentic. Instead of a genuine atavism it seems the fruit of diligent study, burning the midnight oil over a grammar and dictionary.

So in excellent Piedmontese with witty Astian tones he told me he had some sugar he wanted "chemistried": he wanted to know whether it was or was not sugar, or if perhaps there was some "filth" in it. What filth? I explained that if he was more specific about his suspicions it would facilitate my job, but he replied that he didn't want to influence me, that I should make the analysis as best I could, he would tell me about his suspicions later. He left in my hands a paper parcel containing a good half kilo of sugar, told me that he would return the next day, said goodbye, and left: he did not take the elevator but walked calmly down the four flights of stairs. He appeared to be a man without anxieties and without haste.

We didn't have many customers, we didn't make many analyses, and we didn't make much money: so we couldn't buy modern and rapid instruments, our findings were slow, our analyses lasted much longer than normal; we didn't even have a sign on the street, so the circle closed and there were fewer customers yet. The samples left us for analysis constituted a far from negligible contribution toward our sustenance: Emilio and I took care not to let them know that in general a few grams

*In other words, the respectable, subservient middle class. The "illustrious namesake" is the writer, Carlo Levi, who expresses himself on this score quite eloquently

and vividly in his book *The Watch*—TRANS.

was enough and willingly accepted a litre of wine or milk, a kilo of spaghetti or soap, a packet of *agnolotti*.

However, given the patient's history, that is, the old man's suspicions, it would have been imprudent to consume that sugar blindly, even just taste it. I dissolved a little in distilled water: the solution was turbid—there was certainly something wrong with it. I weighed a gram of sugar in the platinum crucible (the apple of our eyes) to incinerate it on the flame: there rose in the lab's polluted air the domestic and childish smell of burnt sugar, but immediately afterward the flame turned livid and there was a much different smell, metallic, garlicky, inorganic, indeed contra-organic: a chemist without a nose is in for trouble. At this point it is hard to make a mistake: filter the solution, acidify it, take the Kipp, let hydrogen sulfide bubble through. And here is the yellow precipitate of sulfide, it is arsenious anhydride—in short, arsenic, the Masculinum, the arsenic of Mithridates and Madame Bovary.

I spent the rest of the day distilling pyruvic acid and speculating on the old man's sugar. I do not know how pyruvic acid is prepared now with modern methods; at that time we melted sulfuric acid and soda in an enameled saucepan, obtaining bisulfate which to solidify we threw on the bare floor, and then ground it in a coffee grinder. Then we heated at 250 degrees centigrade a mixture of the aforementioned bisulfate and tartaric acid, so that the latter dehydrated into pyruvic acid and was distilled. First we attempted this operation in glass receptacles, bursting a prohibitive number; then we bought from a junk man ten metal cannisters, which came from the Allied Army Surplus, the kind which were used for gasoline before the advent of polyethylene, and which proved to be suited to this purpose; since the customer was satisfied with the quality of the product and promised further orders, we took the plunge and had the local blacksmith build a crude cylindrical reactor of sheet iron, equipped with a hand-powered mixer. We set it in a well of solid bricks, which had on the bottom and sides four resistors of 1,000 watts connected illegally upstream to the meter. If a fellow professional is reading this, he should not be too surprised by this pre-Columbian and junk-shop chemistry: during those years we weren't the only ones, nor the only chemists, to live like this, and throughout the world six years of war and destruction had brought about a regression in many civil habits and attenuated many needs, first of all the need for decorum.

From the end of the condenser coil the acid fell into the collector in heavy golden drops, refracting like gems: drop by drop, every ten drops one lira of earnings. And meanwhile I kept thinking of the arsenic and the old man, who did not seem to me the type to plot poisonings or even undergo them, and I couldn't figure it out.

The man returned the next day. He insisted on paying the fee, even before knowing the result of the analysis. When I told him his face lit up with a complicated, wrinkled smile, and he said to me, "I'm glad. I always said it would end up like this." It was evident that he only waited for the slightest solicitation from me to tell the story. I did not disappoint him, and this is the story, a trifle faded due to the translation from Piedmontese, an essentially spoken language.

"I am a cobbler by trade. If you start as a young man, it is not a bad trade: you sit, you don't work hard, and you meet people you can talk to. Certainly you don't make a fortune, you're all day long with other people's shoes in your hands: but you get used to this, even to the smell of old leather. My shop is on Via Gioberti at the corner of Via Pastrengo: I've been working as a cobbler there for thirty years. I am the cobbler of San Secondo; I know all the difficult feet, and to do my work all I need is my hammer and some twine. Well, a young man came, not even from hereabouts: tall, good-looking, and full of ambition; he set up a shop a stone's throw away and filled it with machines. To lengthen, to enlarge, to sew, to hammer out soles, and who knows what else—I never went to look, they told me about it. He put cards with his address and telephone number in all the letter boxes of the neighborhood: yes, sir, even a phone, as if he were a midwife.

"You're sure to think that his business went well right away. It did the first months—a little out of curiosity, a little to give us some competition, some customers went to him; also because at the start he kept his prices low: but then he had to raise them when he saw he was losing money. Now, mind, I'm saying all this without wishing him ill, I've seen plenty like him, starting off at a gallop and breaking their heads, cobblers and not only cobblers. But he, they told me, wished me ill: they tell me everything, and do you know who? The little old ladies, whose feet hurt and who no longer enjoy walking and have only one pair of shoes; they come to me—sit down, waiting for me to take care of the problems, and meanwhile they keep me informed, tell me all the ins and outs.

"He wished me ill and was going around telling a lot of lies about me. That I resoled with cardboard. That I get drunk every night. That I made my wife die for the insurance. That a nail came through the shoe of one of my customers and then he died of tetanus. And so, with things at this point, you can understand that I wasn't surprised too much when one morning, among the day's shoes, I found this parcel. I immediately understood the scheme, but I wanted to make sure: so I gave a little of it to the cat, and after two hours he went in a corner and vomited. Then I put another bit of it in the sugar bowl and yesterday my daughter and I put it in the coffee, and two hours later we both vomited. And now I also have your confirmation and I'm satisfied."

"Do you want to bring charges? Do you need a declaration?"

"No, no. I told you, he's only a poor devil and I don't want to ruin him. For this trade, too, the world is large and there's a place for everyone: he doesn't know it, but I do."

"So?"

"So tomorrow I'll send back the parcel by one of my little old ladies, together with a note. In fact, no—I think I'll bring it back myself, so I can see the face he makes and I'll explain two or three things." He looked around, as one would in a museum, and then added, "Yours too is a fine trade: you need an eye and patience. And he who hasn't got them, it's best that he look for something else."

He said goodbye, picked up the parcel, and walked down without taking the elevator, with the tranquil dignity that was his by nature.

NITROGEN

. . . and finally there came the customer we'd always dreamed of, who wanted us as consultants. To be a consultant is the ideal work, the sort from which you derive prestige and money without dirtying your hands, or breaking your backbone, or running the risk of ending up roasted or poisoned: all you have to do is take off your smock, put on your tie, listen in attentive silence to the problem, and then you'll feel like the Delphic oracle. You must then weigh your reply very carefully and formulate it in convoluted, vague language so that the customer also considers you an oracle, worthy of his faith and the rates set by the Chemists' Society.

The dream client was about forty, small, compact, and obese; he wore a thin mustache like Clark Gable and had tufts of black hairs everywhere—in his ears, inside his nostrils, on the backs of his hands, and on the ridge of his fingers almost down to his fingernails. He was perfumed and pomaded and had a vulgar aspect: he looked like a pimp or, better, a third-rate actor playing the part of a pimp; or a tough from the slummy outskirts. He explained to me that he was the owner of a cosmetics factory and had trouble with a certain kind of lipstick. Good, let him bring us a sample; but no, he said, it was a particular problem, which had to be examined on the spot; it was better for one of us to visit and see what the problem was. Tomorrow at ten? Tomorrow.

It would have been great to show up in a car, but of course if you were a chemist with a car, instead of a miserable returnee, a spare-time writer, and besides just married, you wouldn't spend time here sweating pyruvic acid and chasing after dubious lipstick manufacturers. I put on the best of my (two) suits and thought that it was a good idea to leave my bike in some courtyard nearby and pretend I had arrived in a cab, but when I entered the factory I realized that my scruples about prestige were entirely inappropriate. The factory was a dirty, disorderly shed, full of drafts, in which a dozen impudent, indolent, filthy, and showily made up girls crept about. The owner gave me some explanations, exhibiting pride and trying to look important: he called the lipstick "rouge," the aniline "anelline," and the benzoic aldehyde "adelaide." The work process was simple: a girl melted certain waxes and fats in an ordinary enameled pot, adding a little perfume and a little coloring, then poured the lot into a minuscule ingot mold. Another girl cooled off the molds under running water and extracted from each of the molds twenty small scarlet cylinders of lipstick; other girls took care of the assembly and packing. The owner rudely grabbed one of the girls, put his hand behind her neck to bring her mouth close to my eyes, and invited me to observe carefully the outline of her lips—there, you see, a few hours after application, especially when it's hot, the lipstick runs, it filters up along the very thin lines that even young women have around their lips, and so it forms an ugly web of red threads that blurs the outline and ruins the whole effect.

I peered, not without embarrassment: the red threads were indeed there, but only on the right half of the girl's mouth, as she stood there impassively undergoing the inspection and chewing American gum. Of course, the owner explained: her left side, and the left side of all the other girls, was made up with an excellent French product, in fact the product that he was vainly trying to imitate. A lipstick can be evaluated only in this way, through a practical comparison: every morning all the girls had to make up with the lipstick, on the right with his, and on the left with the other, and he kissed all the girls eight times a day to check whether the product was kiss-proof.

I asked the tough for his lipstick's recipe, and a sample of both products. Reading the recipe, I immediately got the suspicion as to where the defect came from, but it seemed to me more advisable to make certain and let my reply fall a bit from on high, and I requested two days' time "for the analyses." I recovered my bike, and as I pedaled along I thought that, if this business went well, I could perhaps exchange it for a motorbike and quit pedaling.

Back at the lab, I took a sheet of filter paper, made two small red dots with the two samples, and put it in the stove at 80 degrees centigrade. After a quarter of an hour the small dot of the left lipstick was still a dot, although surrounded by a greasy aura, while the small dot of the right lipstick was faded and spread, had become a pinkish halo as large as a coin. In my man's recipe there was a soluble dye; it was clear that, when the heat of the woman's skin (or my stove) caused the fat to melt, the dye followed it as it spread. Instead, the other lipstick must contain a red pigment, well dispersed but insoluble and therefore not migrant: I ascertained this easily by diluting it with benzene and subjecting it to centrifugation, and there it was, deposited on the bottom of the test tube. Thanks to the experience I had accumulated at the lakeshore plant I was able to identify it: it was an expensive pigment and not easy to disperse, and besides, my tough did not have any equipment suited to dispersing pigments. Fine, it was his headache, let him figure it out, him with his harem of girl guinea pigs and his revolting metered kisses. For my part, I had performed my professional services; I made a report, attached an invoice with the necessary tax stamps and the picturesque specimen of filter paper, went back to the factory, handed it over, took my fee, and prepared to say goodbye.

But the tough detained me: he was satisfied with my work and wanted to offer me a business deal. Could I get him a few kilos of alloxan? He would pay a good price for it, provided I committed myself by contract to supply it only to him. He had read, I no longer remember in what magazine, that alloxan in contact with the mucous membrane confers on it an extremely permanent red color, because it is not a superimposition, in short a layer of varnish like lipstick, but a true and proper dye, as used on wool and cotton.

I gulped, and to stay on the safe side replied that we would have to see: alloxan is not a common compound nor very well known, I don't think my old chemistry textbook devoted more than five lines to it, and at that moment I remembered only vaguely that it was a derivative of urea and had some connection with uric acid.

I dashed to the library at the first opportunity; I refer to the venerable library of the University of Turin's Chemical Institute, at that time, like Mecca, impenetrable to infidels and even hard to penetrate for such faithful as I. One had to think that the administration followed the wise principle according to which it is good to discourage the arts and sciences: only someone impelled by absolute necessity, or by an overwhelming passion, would willingly subject himself to the trials of abnegation that were demanded of him in order to consult the volumes. The library's schedule was brief and irrational, the lighting dim, the file cards in disorder; in the winter, no heat; no chairs but uncomfortable and noisy metal stools; and finally, the librarian was an incompetent, insolent boor of exceeding ugliness, stationed at the threshold to terrify with his appearance and his howl those aspiring to enter. Having been let in, I passed the tests, and right away I hastened to refresh my memory as to the composition and structure of alloxan. Here is its portrait:

in which O is oxygen, C is carbon, H hydrogen, and N nitrogen. It is a pretty structure, isn't it? It makes you think of something solid, stable, well linked. In fact it happens also in chemistry as in architecture that "beautiful" edifices, that is, symmetrical and simple, are also the most sturdy: in short, the same thing happens with molecules as with the cupolas of cathedrals or the arches of bridges. And it is also possible that the explanation is neither remote nor metaphysical: to say "beautiful" is to say "desirable," and ever since man has built he has wanted to build at the smallest expense and in the most durable fashion, and the aesthetic enjoyment he experiences when contemplating his work comes afterward. Certainly, it has not always been this way: there have been centuries in which "beauty" was identified with adornment, the superimposed, the frills; but it is probable that they were deviant epochs and that the true beauty, in which every century recognizes itself, is found in upright stones, ships' hulls, the blade of an ax, the wing of a plane.

Having recognized and appreciated the structural virtue of alloxan, it is urgent that my chemical alter ego, so in love with digressions, get back on the rails, which is that of fornicating with matter in order to support myself—and today, not just myself. I turned with respect to the shelves of the *Zentralblatt* and began to consult it year by year. Hats off to the *Chemisches Zentralblatt*: it is the magazine of magazines, the magazine which, ever since Chemistry existed, has reported in the form of   *179* furiously concise abstracts all the articles dealing with chemistry that appear in all the magazines in the world. The first years are slender volumes of 300 or 400 pages: today, every year, they dish out fourteen volumes of 1,300 pages each. It is endowed with a majestic authors' index, one for subjects, one for formulas, and you can find in it venerable fossils, such as the legendary memoir in which our father Wöhler tells the story of the first organic synthesis or Sainte-Claire Deville describes the first isolation of metallic aluminum.

From the *Zentralblatt* I ricocheted to *Beilstein*, an equally monumental encyclopedia continually brought up to date in which, as in an Office of Records, each new chemical compound is described as it appears, together with its methods of preparation. Alloxan was known for almost seventy years, but as a laboratory curiosity: the preparation method described had a pure academic value, and proceeded from expensive raw materials which (in those years right after the war) it was vain to hope to find on the market. The sole accessible preparation was the oldest: it did not seem too difficult to execute, and consisted in an oxidizing demolition of uric acid. Just that: uric acid, the stuff connected with gout, intemperant eaters, and stones in the bladder. It was a decidedly unusual raw material, but perhaps not as prohibitively expensive as the others.

In fact subsequent research in the spick and span shelves, smelling of camphor, wax, and century-old chemical labors, taught me that uric acid, very scarce in the excreta of man and mammals, constitutes, however, 50 percent of the excrement of birds and 90 percent of the excrement of reptiles. Fine. I phoned the tough and told him that it could be done, he just had to give me a few days' time: before the month was out I would bring him the first sample of alloxan, and give him an idea of the cost and how much of it I could produce each month. The fact that alloxan, destined to embellish ladies' lips, would come from the excrement of chickens or pythons was a thought which didn't trouble me for a moment. The trade of chemist (fortified, in my case, by the experience of Auschwitz) teaches you to overcome, indeed to ignore, certain revulsions that are neither necessary or congenital: matter is matter, neither noble nor vile, infinitely transformable, and its proximate origin is of no importance whatsoever. Nitrogen is nitrogen, it passes miraculously from the air into plants, from these into animals, and from animals to us; when its function in our body is exhausted, we eliminate it, but it still remains nitrogen, aseptic, innocent. We—I mean to say we mammals—who in general do not have problems about obtaining water, have learned to wedge it into the urea molecule, which is soluble in water, and as urea we free ourselves of it; other animals, for whom water is precious (or it was for their distant progenitors), have made the ingenious invention of packaging their nitrogen in the form of uric acid, which is insoluble in water, and of eliminating it as a solid, with no necessity of having recourse to water as a vehicle. In an analogous fashion one thinks today of eliminating urban garbage by pressing it into blocks, which can be carried to the dumps or buried inexpensively.

I will go further: far from scandalizing me, the idea of obtaining a cosmetic from excrement, that is, *aurum de stercore* ("gold from dung"), amused me and warmed my heart like a return to the origins, when alchemists extracted phosphorus from urine. It was an adventure both unprecedented and gay and noble besides, because it ennobled, restored, and reestablished. That is what nature does: it draws the fern's grace from the putrefaction of the forest floor, and pasturage from manure, in Latin *laetamen*—and does not *laetari* mean "to rejoice"? That's what they taught me in *liceo*, that's how it had been for Virgil, and that's what it became for me. I returned home that evening, told my very recent wife the story of the alloxan and uric acid, and informed her that the next day I would leave on a business trip: that is, I would get on my bike and make a tour of the farms on the outskirts of town (at that time they were still there) in search of chicken shit. She did not hesitate; she likes the countryside, and a wife should follow her husband; she would come along with me. It was a kind of supplement to our honeymoon trip, which for reasons of economy had been frugal and hurried. But she warned me not to have too many illusions: finding chicken shit in its pure state would not be so easy.

In fact it proved quite difficult. First of all, the *pollina*—that's what the country people call it, which we didn't know, nor did we know that, because of its nitrogen content, it is highly valued as a fertilizer for truck gardens—the chicken shit is not given away free, indeed it is sold at a high price. Secondly, whoever buys it has to go and gather it, crawling on all fours into the chicken coops and gleaning all around the threshing floor. And thirdly, what you actually collect can be used directly as a fertilizer, but lends itself badly to other uses: it is a mixture of dung, earth, stones, chicken feed, feathers, and chicken lice, which nest under the chickens' wings. In any event, paying not a little, laboring and dirtying ourselves a lot, my undaunted wife and I returned that evening down Corso Francia with a kilo of sweated-over chicken shit on the bike's carrier rack.

The next day I examined the material: there was a lot of gangue, yet something perhaps could be gotten from it. But simultaneously I got an idea; just at that time, in the Turin subway gallery an exhibition of snakes had opened: Why not go and see it? Snakes are a clean species, they have neither feathers nor lice, and they don't scrabble in the dirt; and besides, a python is quite a bit larger than a chicken. Perhaps their excrement, at 90 percent uric acid, could be obtained in abundance, in sizes not too minute and in conditions of reasonable purity. This time I went alone: my wife is a daughter of Eve and doesn't like snakes.

The director and the various workers attached to the exhibition received me with stupefied scorn. Where were my credentials? Where did I come from? Who did I think I was showing up just like that, as if it were the most natural thing, asking for python shit? Out of the question, not even a gram; pythons are frugal, they eat twice a month and vice versa; especially when they don't get much exercise. Their very scanty shit is worth its weight in gold; besides, they—and all exhibitors and owners of snakes—have permanent and exclusive contracts with big pharmaceutical companies. So get out and stop wasting our time.

I devoted a day to a coarse sifting of the chicken shit, and another two trying to oxidize the acid contained in it into alloxan. The virtue and patience of ancient chemists must have been superhuman, or perhaps my inexperience with organic preparations was boundless. All I got were foul vapors, boredom, humiliation, and a black and murky liquid which irremediably plugged up the filters and displayed no tendency to crystallize, as the text declared it should. The shit remained shit, and the alloxan and its resonant name remained a resonant name. That was not the way to get out of the swamps: by what path would I therefore get out, I the discouraged author of a book which seemed good to me but which nobody read? Best to return among the colorless but safe schemes of inorganic chemistry.

TIN

It's bad to be poor, I was brooding as I held an ingot of tin from the Straits over the flame of the gas jet. Very slowly the tin melted, and the drops fell with a hiss into the water of a basin: on the basin's bottom a fascinating metallic tangle of ever new shapes was forming.

There are friendly metals and hostile metals. Tin was a friend—not only because, for some months now, Emilio and I were living on it, transforming it into stannous chloride to sell to the manufacturers of mirrors, but also for other, more recondite reasons: because it marries with iron, transforming it into mild tin plate and depriving it on that account of its sanguinary quality of *nocens ferrum*; because the Phoenicians traded in it and it is to this day extracted, refined, and shipped from fabulous and distant countries (the Straits, precisely: one might say the Sleepy Sonda Islands, the Happy Isles and Archipelagos); because it forms an alloy with copper to give us bronze, the respectable material par excellence, notoriously perennial and well established; because it melts at a low temperature, almost like organic compounds, that is, almost like us; and finally, because of two unique properties with picturesque, hardly credible names, never seen or heard (that I know) by human eye or ear, yet faithfully handed down from generation to generation by all the textbooks—the "weeping" of tin and tin pest.

You have to granulate tin so that afterward it can be easier to attack with hydrochloric acid. So you asked for it. You were living under the wings of that lakeshore factory, a bird of prey but with broad, strong wings. You decided to get out from under its protection, fly with your own wings: well, you asked for it. So fly now: you wanted to be free and you are free, you wanted to be a chemist and you are one. So now grub among poisons, lipsticks, and chicken shit; granulate tin, pour hydrochloric acid; concentrate, decant, and crystallize if you do not want to go hungry, and you know hunger. Buy tin and sell stannous chloride.

Emilio had managed to carve a lab out of his parents' apartment, pious, ill-advised, long-suffering people. Certainly, when they let him take over their bedroom, they had not foreseen all the consequences, but there's no way back: now the hallway was a storeroom jammed with demijohns full of concentrated hydrochloric acid, the kitchen stove (outside of mealtime) was used to concentrate the stannous chloride in beakers and six-liter Erlenmeyer flasks, and the entire apartment was invaded with our fumes.

Emilio's father was a majestic, benign old man with a white mustache and a thunderous voice. He had had many different trades during his life, all adventurous or at least odd, and at seventy he still had a preoccupying avidity for experimentation. At that period he held the monopoly of the blood of all the 185 cattle slaughtered at the old Municipal Slaughterhouse on Corso Inghilterra: he spent many hours of the day in a filthy cavern, its walls brown from dried-up blood, its floor soaked with putrified muck, and frequented by rats as large as rabbits; even his invoices and ledgers were stained with blood. The blood was turned into buttons, glue, fritters, blood sausages, wall paints, and polishing paste. He read exclusively Arabic newspapers and magazines, which he had sent from Cairo, where he had lived many years, where he had had three sons, where he had defended, rifle in hand, the Italian Consulate from an enraged mob, and where his heart remained. He went every day on his bicycle to Porta Palazzo to buy herbs, sorghum flour, peanut fat, and sweet potatoes: with these ingredients and the slaughterhouse blood he cooked experimental dishes, a different one each day; he bragged about them and made us taste them. One day he brought home a rat, cut off its head and paws, told his wife that it was a guinea pig, and had her roast it. Since his bicycle did not have a guard over the chain and the small of his back had become a bit stiff, he would put clips on the cuffs of his pants in the morning and wouldn't take them off all day. He and his wife, the sweet and imperturbable Signora Ester, born in Corfu of a Venetian family, had accepted our laboratory in their house, as if keeping acids in the kitchen was the most natural thing in the world. We would carry the demijohns of acid to the fourth floor in the elevator; Emilio's father looked so respectable and authoritative that no tenant dared object.

Our laboratory looked like a junk shop and the hold of a whaler. Apart from overflows that, as I said, invaded the kitchen, the hallway, and even the bathroom, the lab consisted of a single room and the terrace. On the terrace were scattered the parts of a DKW motorcycle which Emilio had bought dismantled and which, he said, he would put together again someday; the scarlet gas tank was perched on the railing, and the motor, inside a fly net, rusted away, corroded by our exhalations. There were also some tanks of ammonia left over from an epoch preceding my arrival, during which Emilio made ends meet by dissolving gaseous ammonia in demijohns of potable water, selling them, and befouling the neighborhood. Everywhere, on the terrace and inside the apartment, was scattered an incredible amount of junk, so old and battered as to prove almost unrecognizable: only after a more attentive examination could you distinguish the professional objects from the domestic ones.

In the middle of the lab was a large ventilation hood of wood and glass, our pride and our only protection against death by gasing. It is not that hydrochloric acid is actually toxic: it is one of those frank enemies that come at you shouting from a distance, and from which it is therefore easy to protect yourself. It has such a penetrating odor that whoever can wastes no time in getting out of its way; and you cannot mistake it for anything else, because after having taken in one breath of it you expel from your nose two short plumes of white smoke, like the horses in Eisenstein's movies, and you feel your teeth turn sour in your mouth, as when you have bitten into a lemon. Despite our quite willing hood, acid fumes invaded all the rooms: the wallpaper changed color, the doorknobs and metal fixtures became dim and rough, and every so often a sinister thump made us jump: a nail had been corroded through and a picture, in some corner of the apartment, had crashed to the floor. Emilio hammered in a new nail and hung the picture back in its place.

So we were dissolving tin in hydrochloric acid: then the solution had to be concentrated to a particular specific weight and left to crystallize by cooling. The stannous chloride separated in small, pretty prisms, colorless and transparent. Since the crystallization was slow, it required many receptacles, and since hydrochloric acid corrodes all metals, these receptacles had to be glass or ceramic. In the period when there were many orders, we had to mobilize reserve receptacles, in which for that matter Emilio's house was rich: a soup tureen, an enameled iron pressure cooker, an Art Nouveau chandelier, and a chamber pot.

The morning after, the chloride is gathered and set to drain: *187* and you must be very careful not to touch it with your hands or it saddles you with a truly disgusting smell. This salt, in itself, is odorless, but it reacts in some manner with the skin, perhaps reducing the keratin's dissulfide bridges and giving off a persistent metallic stench that for several days announces to all that you are a chemist. It is aggressive but also delicate, like certain unpleasant sports opponents who whine when they lose: you can't force it, you have to let it dry out in the air in its own good time. If you try to warm it up, even in the mildest manner, for example, with a hair dryer or on the radiator, it loses its crystallization water, becomes opaque, and foolish customers no longer want it. Foolish because it would suit them fine: with less water there is more tin and therefore more of a yield; but that's how it is, the customer is always right, especially when he knows little chemistry, as is precisely the case with mirror manufacturers.

Nothing of the generous good nature of tin, Jove's metal, survives in its chloride (besides, chlorides in general are rabble, for the most part ignoble by-products, hygroscopic, not good for much: with the single exception of common salt, which is a completely different matter). This salt is an energetic reducing agent, that is to say, it is eager to free itself of two of its electrons and does so on the slightest pretext, sometimes with disastrous results: just a single splash of the concentrated solution, which dripped down my pants, was enough to cut them cleanly like the blow of a scimitar; and this was right after the war, and I had no other pants except my Sunday best, and there wasn't much money in the house.

I would never have left the lakeshore factory, and I would have stayed there for all eternity correcting varnishes' deformities, if Emilio had not insisted, praising adventure and the glories of a free profession. I had quit my job with absurd self-assurance, distributing to my colleagues and superiors a testament written in quatrains full of gay impudence: I was quite aware of the risk I was running, but I knew that the license to make mistakes becomes more limited with the passing of the years, so he who wants to take advantage of it must not wait too long. On the other hand, one must not wait too long to realize that a mistake is a mistake: at the end of each month we did our accounts, and it was becoming ever more obvious that man does not live by stannous chloride alone; or at least I did not, since I had just married and had no authoritative patriarch behind me.

We didn't surrender right away; we racked our brains for a good month in an effort to obtain vanillin from eugenol with an output that would permit us to live, and didn't succeed; we secreted several hundred kilos of pyruvic acid, produced with equipment for troglodytes and a work schedule for slaves, after which I hoisted the white flag. I had to find a job, even if it meant going back to varnishes.

Emilio accepted the common defeat and my desertion with sorrow but like a man. For him it was different: in his veins ran the paternal blood, rich in remote piratic ferments, mercantile initiatives, and a restless frenzy for the new. He was not afraid of making mistakes, nor of changing his trade, the place, and the style of his life every six months, nor of becoming poor; nor did he have any caste hang-ups, nor did he feel ill at ease about going around on his tricycle and in gray overalls to deliver our laborious chloride to customers. He accepted, and the next day he already had in mind other ideas, other deals with people more experienced than I, and immediately set about dismantling the laboratory, and he wasn't even all that sad, whereas I was and felt like crying, or of howling at the moon as dogs do when they see the suitcases being closed. We proceeded to carry out the melancholy task helped (or, better, distracted and impeded) by Signor Samuele and Signora Ester. There came to light family utensils, sought in vain for years, and other exotic objects, buried geologically in the apartment's recesses: the breechblock of a Beretta 38 tommy gun (from the days when Emilio had been a partisan and roamed the mountain valleys, distributing spare parts to the bands), an illuminated Koran, a very long porcelain pipe, a damascened sword with a hilt inlaid with silver, and an avalanche of yellowed papers. Among these rose to the surface—and I appropriated it greedily—a proclamation decree of 1785 in which F. Tom. Lorenzo Matteucci, General Inquisitor of the Ancona District, especially delegated against the heretical depravity, with much complacency and little clarity, "orders, prohibits, and severely commands, that no Jew shall have the temerity to take Lessons from Christians for any kind of Instrument, and much less that of Dancing." We put off until the next day the most anguishing job, the dismantling of the ventilation hood.

Despite Emilio's opinion, it was immediately clear that our efforts would not be sufficient. It was painful to draft a couple of carpenters, whom Emilio ordered to build a contraption fit to uproot the hood from its anchorage without dismembering it: in sum, this hood was a symbol, the sign of a profession and condition, indeed an art, and should have been deposited in the courtyard intact and in its integrity, so as to find a new life and use in a still undefined future.

A scaffolding was built, a block and tackle were set up, and guide ropes were strung. While Emilio and I watched the funereal ceremony from the courtyard, the hood issued solemnly from the window, hovered ponderously, outlined sharply against the gray sky of Via Massena, was skillfully hooked onto the chain of the block and tackle, and the chain groaned once and broke. The hood plunged four floors to our feet and was reduced to shards of wood and glass; it still smelled of eugenol and pyruvic acid, and with it our will and daring for enterprise was also reduced to shards.

In the brief instants of the flight the instinct of self-preservation made us take a leap backward. Emilio said, "I thought it would make more noise."

URANIUM

One cannot employ just anyone to do the work of Customers' Service. It is a delicate and complex job, not much different from that of diplomats: to perform it with success you must infuse faith in the customers, and therefore it is indispensable to have faith in yourself and in the products you sell; it is therefore a salutary activity, which helps you to know yourself and strengthens your character. It is perhaps the most hygienic of the specialities that constitute the decathlon of the factory chemist: the speciality that best trains him in eloquence and improvisation, prompt reflexes, and the ability to understand and make yourself understood; besides, you get a chance to travel about Italy and the world, and it brings you into contact with all sorts of people. I must also mention another peculiar and beneficent consequence of CS: by pretending to esteem and like your fellow men, after a few years in this trade you wind up really doing so, just as someone who feigns madness for a long time actually becomes crazy.

In the majority of cases, at the first contact you have to acquire or conquer a position superior to that of your interlocutor: but conquer it quietly, graciously, without frightening him or pulling rank. He must feel you are superior, but just a little: reachable, comprehensible. Never, but never, for instance, talk chemistry with a non-chemist: this is the ABC of the trade. But the opposite danger is much more serious, that the customer outranks you: and this can easily happen, because he plays at home, that is, he puts the products you're selling him to practical use, and so he knows their virtues and defects as a wife knows her husband's, while usually you have only a painless, disinterested, often optimistic knowledge of them, acquired in the lab or during their production. The most favorable constellation is that in which you can present yourself as a benefactor, in whatever way: by convincing him that your product satisfies an old need or desire of his, perhaps overlooked; that, having taken everything into account, at the end of the year it would prove to cost less than the competition's product, which moreover, as is known, works well at first but, well, I don't really want to go into it. You can, however, assist him also in different ways (and here the imagination of the CS candidate is revealed): by solving a technical problem for him that has little or nothing to do with your business: furnishing him with an address; inviting him to dinner in a typical restaurant; showing him your city and helping him or advising him on the purchase of souvenirs for his wife or girlfriend; finding him at the last moment a ticket in the stadium for the local soccer match (that's right, we do this too). My Bologna colleague has a collection of dirty stories continually brought up to date, and reviews them diligently together with the technical bulletins before setting out on his sales trip in the cities and provinces; since he has a faulty memory, he keeps a record of which he has told to whom, because to administer the same joke twice to the same person would be a serious mistake.

All these things are learned through experience, but there are technical salesmen who seem born to it, born CS like Athena. This is not my case, and I am sadly conscious of it: when it falls to me to work in CS, at the office or traveling, I do it unwillingly, with hesitation, compunction, and little human warmth. Worse: I tend to be brusque and impatient with customers who are impatient and brusque, and to be mild and yielding with suppliers who, being in their turn CSs, prove to be just that, yielding and mild. In short, I am not a good CS, and I fear that by now it is too late for me to become one.

Tabasso had said to me, "Go to _____ and ask for Bonino, who is the head of the department. He's a fine man, already knows our products, everything has always gone well, he's no genius, we haven't called on him for three months. You will see that you won't have any technical difficulties; and if he begins to talk prices, just keep to generalities: tell him that you'll report to us and it's not your job . . ."

I had myself announced; they gave me a form to fill out and handed me a badge to stick to my lapel, which characterized you as an outsider and immunized you against reactions of rejection on the part of the guards. They had me sit down in a waiting room; after not more than five minutes Bonino appeared and led me to his office. This is an excellent sign, and it doesn't always go like this: there are people who, coldly, make a CS wait for thirty or forty minutes even if there is an appointment, with the deliberate aim of putting him down and imposing their superior rank; it is the same goal aimed at, with more ingenious and more obscene techniques, by the baboons in the big ditch in the zoo. But the analogy is more general: all of a CS's strategies and tactics can be described in terms of sexual courtship. In both cases it's a one-to-one relationship; a courtship or negotiation among three persons would be unthinkable. In both cases one notes at the beginning a kind of dance or ritualized opening in which the buyer accepts the seller only if the latter adheres rigidly to the traditional ceremonial; if this takes place, the buyer joins the dance, and if the enjoyment is mutual, mating is attained, that is, the purchase, to the visible satisfaction of the two partners. The cases of unilateral violence are rare; not by chance are they often described in terms borrowed from the sexual sphere.

Bonino was a round little man, untidy, vaguely canine, carelessly shaved, and with a toothless smile. I introduced myself and initiated the propitiatory dance, but right off he said, "Ah yes, you're the fellow who wrote a book." I must confess my weakness: this irregular opening does not displease me, although it is not very useful to the company I represent; indeed, at this point the conversation tends to degenerate, or at least lose itself in anomalous considerations, which distract from the purpose of the visit and waste professional time.

"It's really a fine novel," Bonino continued. "I read it during my vacation, and I also got my wife to read it; but not the children, because it might frighten them." These opinions usually irritate me, but when one is in the CS role one must not be too discriminating: I thanked him urbanely and tried to bring the conversation back on the proper tracks, that is, our varnishes. Bonino put up some resistance.

"Just as you see me, I also risked finishing up like you did. They had already shut me up in the barrack's courtyard, on Corso Orbassano: but at a certain point I saw him come in, you know very well who I mean, and then, while nobody saw me, I climbed the wall, threw myself down on the other side, which was a good five meters, and took off. Then I went to Val Susa with the Badogliani."*

I had never heard a Badogliano call the Badogliani Badogliani, I set up my defenses and, in fact, caught myself taking a deep breath, as someone does when preparing for a long immersion.

*The group, after the collapse of Mussolini's government in September 1943, that
194 supported General Badoglio, who in turn supported the King—TRANS.

It was clear that Bonino's story would be far from brief: but I remembered how many long stories I myself had inflicted on people, on those who wanted to listen and those who didn't. I remembered that it is written (Deuteronomy 10:19): "Love ye therefore the stranger: for ye were strangers in the land of Egypt," and I settled back comfortably in my chair.

Bonino was not a good storyteller: he roamed, repeated himself, made long digressions, and digressions inside digressions. Besides, he had the curious bad habit of omitting the subject of some sentences and replacing it with a personal pronoun, which rendered his discourse even more nebulous. As he was speaking, I distractedly examined the room where he had received me: evidently his office for many years, because it looked neglected and untidy like him. The windows were offensively dirty, the walls were grimy with soot, the gloomy smell of stale tobacco stagnated in the air. Rusty nails were driven into the walls: some apparently useless, others holding up yellowed sheets. One of these, which could be read from my observation post, began like this: "SUBJECT: Rags. With ever greater frequency. . . ." Elsewhere you could see used razor blades, soccer pool slips, medical insurance forms, picture postcards.

". . . so then he told me that I should walk behind him, no in fact ahead of him: it was he who was behind me, a pistol pointed at me. Then the other guy arrived, his crony, who was waiting for him around the corner; and between the two of them they took me to Via Asti, you know what I mean, where there was Aloisio Smit. He would send for me every so often and say talk talk because your pals have already talked and there's no point playing the hero. . . ."

On Bonino's desk there was a horrible reproduction in a light alloy of the Leaning Tower of Pisa. There was also an ashtray made from a seashell, full of cigarette butts and cherry pits, and an alabaster penholder shaped like Vesuvius. It was a pathetic desk, not more than 0.6 square meters at a generous estimate. There is not a seasoned CS who does not know this sad science of the desk: perhaps not at a conscious level, but in the form of a conditioned reflex, a scanty desk inexorably proclaims a lowly occupant; as for that clerk who, within eight or ten days after being hired, has not been able to conquer a desk, well, he is a lost man: he cannot count on more than a few weeks' survival, like a hermit crab without a shell. On the other hand, I have known people who at the end of their careers disposed of a surface of seven or eight square meters with a polyester gloss, obviously excessive but a proper expression in code of the extent of their power. What objects rest on the desk is not important quantitatively: there is the man who expresses his authority by maintaining on its surface the greatest disorder and the greatest accumulation of stationery; there is on the contrary the man who, more subtly, imposes his rank by a void and meticulous cleanliness: that's what Mussolini did, so they say, at Palazzo Venezia.

". . . but all these men were not aware that in my belt I had a pistol too. When they began to torture me, I pulled it out, made them all stand facing the wall, and I got out. But he . . ."

He who? I was perplexed; the story was getting more and more garbled, the clock was running, and though it is true that the customer is always right, there's also a limit to selling one's soul and to fidelity to the company's orders: beyond this limit you make yourself ridiculous.

". . . as far as I could: a half hour, and I was already in the Rivoli section. I was walking along the road, and there what do I see landing in the fields nearby but a German plane, a Stork, the kind that can land in fifty meters. Two men get out, very polite, and ask me please which way to Switzerland. I happen to know these places and I answered right off: straight ahead, like that, to Milan and then turn left. 'Danke,' they answer, and get back in the plane; then one of them has a second thought, rummages under his seat, gets out, and comes over to me holding something like a rock in his hand; he hands it to me and says, 'This is for your trouble: take good care of it, it's uranium.' You understand, it was the end of the war, by now they felt lost, they no longer had the time to make the atomic bomb and they didn't need uranium anymore. They thought only of saving their skins and escaping to Switzerland."

There is also a limit to how much you can control your facial muscles: Bonino must have caught some sign on my face of incredulity, because he broke off in a slightly offended tone and said, "Don't you believe me?"

"Of course I believe you," I responded heroically. "But was it really uranium?"

"Absolutely: anyone could have seen that. It had an incredible weight, and when you touched it, it was hot. Besides, I still have it at home: I keep it on the terrace in a little shed, a secret, so the kids can't touch it; every so often I show it to my friends, and it's remained hot, it's hot even now." He hesitated a moment, then added, "You know what I'll do? Tomorrow I'll send you a piece so you'll be convinced, and maybe, since you're a writer, along with your stories one of these days you'll also write this one."

I thanked him, dutifully did my number, explained a certain new product, took a rather large order, said goodbye, and considered the case closed. But the next day, on my 1.2-square-meter desk, sat a small package addressed to my attention. I opened it, not without curiosity: it contained a small block of metal, about half a cigarette pack in size, actually quite heavy and with an exotic look about it. The surface was silvery white, with a light yellowish glaze: it did not seem hot, but it was not to be confused with any of the metals that a long everyday experience also outside chemistry had made familiar to me, such as copper, zinc, and aluminum. Perhaps an alloy? Or perhaps actually uranium? Metallic uranium in our parts has never been seen by anyone, and in the treatises it is described as silvery white; and a small block like that would not be permanently hot: perhaps only a mass as big as a house can remain hot at the expense of disintegrating energy.

As soon as it was decently possible I popped into the lab, which for a CS chemist is an unusual and vaguely improper *197* thing to do. The lab is a place for the young, and returning there you feel young again: with the same longing for adventure, discovery, and the unexpected that you have at seventeen. Of course, you haven't been seventeen for some time now, and besides, your long career as a para-chemist has mortified you, rendered you atrophied, handicapped, kept you ignorant as to where reagents and equipment are stored, forgetful of everything except the fundamental reactions: but precisely for these reasons the lab revisited is a source of joy and exerts an intense fascination, which is that of youth, of an indeterminate future pregnant with possibilities, that is, of freedom.

But the years of non-use don't make you forget certain professional tics, a certain stereotyped behavior that marks you out as a chemist whatever the situation: probing the unknown material with your fingernail, a penknife, smelling it, feeling it with your lips whether it is "cold" or "hot," testing whether it scratches the windowpane or not, observing it under reflected light, weighing it in the palm of your hand. It is not so easy to estimate the specific weight of a material without a scale, yet after all uranium has a specific weight of 19, much more than lead, twice as much as copper: the gift given to Bonino by the Nazi aeronaut-astronauts could not be uranium. I was beginning to discern, in the little man's paranoic tale, the echo of a tenacious and recurrent local legend of UFOs in the Val Susa, of flying saucers, carriers of omens like the comets in the Middle Ages, erratic and devoid of results like the spirits of the spiritualists.

But if it wasn't uranium, what was it? I cut off a slice of the metal with the handsaw (it was easy to saw) and offered it to the flame of the Bunsen burner: an unusual thing took place: a thread of brown smoke rose from the flame, a thread which curled into volutes. I felt, with an instant of voluptuous nostalgia, reawaken in me the reflexes of an analyst, withered by long inertia: I found a capsule of enameled porcelain, filled it with water, held it over the sooty flame, and saw form on the bottom a brown deposit which was an old acquaintance. I touched the deposit with a drop of silver nitrate solution and the black-blue color that developed confirmed for me that the metal was cadmium, the distant son of Cadmus, the sower of dragon's teeth.

Where Bonino had found the cadmium was not very interesting: probably in the cadmium-plating department of his factory. More interesting but undecipherable was the origin of his story: profoundly his, his alone, since, as I found out later, he told it often and to everyone, but without substantiating it with the support of material, and with details that gradually became more colorful and less believable with the passing of the years. It was clearly impossible to get to the bottom of it: but I, tangled in the CS net of duties toward society, the company, and verisimilitude, envied in him the boundless freedom of invention of one who has broken through the barrier and is now free to build for himself the past that suits him best, to stitch around him the garments of a hero and fly like Superman across centuries, meridians, and parallels.

SILVER

A mimeographed circular is generally tossed into the wastebasket without even being read, but I realized immediately that this one did not deserve the common fate: it was an invitation to a dinner celebrating the twenty-fifth anniversary of our graduation from college. Its language got me to thinking: the addressee was treated to the intimate *tu*, and the amanuensis paraded a series of outdated student expressions, as if those twenty-five years had not passed. With involuntary comedy, the text concluded by saying, ". . . in an atmosphere of renewed comradeship, we will celebrate our silver wedding with Chemistry by telling each other the chemical events of our everyday life." What chemical events? The precipitation of sterols in our fifty-year-old arteries? The equilibrium of membrane in our membranes?

Who could the author be? I mentally passed in review my surviving twenty-five or thirty classmates: I mean to say not only those alive but those who have not disappeared behind the headland of other professional activities. First of all, cross off all the women: all mothers of families, all demobilized, none of them any longer in possession of "events" to be narrated. Cross off the climbers, the climbing, the protégés, the ex-protégés turned protectors: these are people who do not like comparisons. Cross off the frustrated, too, who do not like comparisons either: at a meeting of this kind a shipwrecked man might even show up, but only to solicit sympathy or help; it is unlikely that he would take the initiative to organize it. From the meager list that was left a probable name popped up: Cerrato—the honest, clumsy, eager Cerrato, to whom life had given so little and who had given so little to life. I had met him at intervals and fleetingly after the war, and he was an inert man, not shipwrecked: a shipwrecked man is he who departs and sinks, who sets himself a goal, does not reach it, and suffers because of it; Cerrato had never set himself anything, he had not exposed himself to anything, he had remained safely shut up in his house, and certainly must have clung to the "golden" years of his studies since all his other years had been years of lead.

Faced by the prospect of that dinner I had a two-sided reaction: it was not a neutral event, it attracted and repelled me at the same time, like a magnet brought close to a compass. I wanted to go and I didn't want to: but the motivations for both decisions, closely examined, were not very noble. I wanted to go because it flattered me to compare myself to and feel myself more available than the others, less tied to money and the common idols, less duped, less worn out. I did not want to go because I did not want to be the same age as the others, that is, my age: I didn't want to see wrinkles, white hair, didn't want to count how many we were, nor count the absent, nor go in for calculations.

And yet Cerrato aroused my curiosity. At times we had studied together: he was serious and had no indulgence for himself, he studied without inspiration and without joy (he did not seem to know joy), successively boring through the chapters of the texts like a miner in a tunnel. He had not been compromised by Fascism, and he had reacted well to the reagent of the racial laws. He had been an opaque but reliable boy in whom one could trust: and experience teaches us that just this, trustworthiness, is the most constant virtue, which is not acquired or lost with the years. One is born worthy of trust, with an open face and steady eyes, and remains such for life. He who is born contorted and lax remains that way: he who lies to you at six, lies to you at sixteen and sixty. The phenomenon is striking and explains how certain friendships and marriages survive for several decades, despite habit, boredom, and the wearing out of subjects of discussion: I was interested in verifying this through Cerrato. I paid my contribution and wrote to the anonymous committee that I would be at the dinner.

His appearance hadn't changed very much: he was tall, bony, with an olive complexion; his hair was still thick, his face well shaven, his forehead, nose, and chin heavy, as if roughly molded. Now as then he moved awkwardly, with those abrupt and at the same time uncertain gestures which in the lab had made him the proverbial smasher of glassware.

As is the custom we dedicated the first minutes of our conversation to a reciprocal bringing up to date. I learned that he was married without children, and simultaneously understood that this was not an agreeable subject. I learned that he had always worked in photographic chemistry: ten years in Italy, four in Germany, then again in Italy. He had, yes, been the promoter of the dinner and the author of the letter of invitation. He was not ashamed to admit it; if I would allow him a professional metaphor, his years of study were his Technicolor, the remainder was black and white. As to the "events" (I kept myself from pointing out to him the clumsiness of this expression), they really interested him. His career had been rich in events, even if for the most part they had indeed only been in black and white: Was that true of mine too? Of course, I agreed: whether chemical or not, though in recent years the chemical events had prevailed, in frequency and intensity. They give you a sense of *Nicht dazu gewachsen*, of impotence, inadequacy, isn't that so? They give you the impression of fighting an interminable war against an obtuse and slow-moving enemy, who, however, is fearful in terms of number and bulk; of losing all the battles, one after the other, year after year; and to salve your bruised pride you must be satisfied with the few occasions when you catch sight of a break in the enemy front and you pounce on it and administer a quick single blow.

Cerrato also knew this never-ending battle: he too had experienced the inadequacy of our preparation, and the need to make up for it with luck, intuition, stratagems, and a river of patience. I told him that I was in search of events, mine and those of others, which I wanted to put on display in a book, to see if I could convey to the layman the strong and bitter flavor of our trade, which is only a particular instance, a more strenuous version of the business of living. I told him that it did not seem fair to me that the world should know everything about how the doctor, prostitute, sailor, assassin, countess, ancient Roman, conspirator, and Polynesian lives and nothing about how we transformers of matter live: but that in this book I would deliberately neglect the grand chemistry, the triumphant chemistry of colossal plants and dizzying output, because this is collective work and therefore anonymous. I was more interested in the stories of the solitary chemistry, unarmed and on foot, at the measure of man, which with few exceptions has been mine: but it has also been the chemistry of the founders, who did not work in teams but alone, surrounded by the indifference of their time, generally without profit, and who confronted matter without aids, with their brains and hands, reason and imagination.

I asked him if he would like to contribute to this book. If he would, he should tell me a story and, if he would allow me to make a suggestion, it should be our kind of story, in which you thrash about in the dark for a week or a month, it seems that it will be dark forever, and you feel like throwing it all up and changing your trade; then in the dark you espy a glimmer, proceed groping in that direction, and the light grows, and finally order follows chaos. Cerrato said seriously that indeed sometimes things went like that, and that he would try to come up with something; but in general it was really dark all the time. You couldn't see the glimmer, you beat your head again and again against an ever lower ceiling, and ended by coming out of the cave on your hands and knees and backward, a little older than when you went in. While he was interrogating his memory, his gaze fixed on the restaurant's presumptuously frescoed ceiling, I took a quick glance at him and saw that he had aged well, without deformations, on the contrary growing and maturing: he had remained heavy, as in the past, incapable of the refreshment of malice and laughter, but this was no longer offensive, and more acceptable in a fifty-year-old than in a youth of twenty. He told me a story of silver.

"I'll tell you the essentials: the trimmings you can put in yourself—for example, how an Italian lives in Germany; after all, you've been there yourself. I was in charge of the department where they manufactured the papers for X-rays. Do you know anything about that stuff? Never mind: it's not very sensitive material, which doesn't give you trouble (sensitivity and trouble are proportional): so the department was also rather tranquil. But you must remember that if a film for amateurs functions badly, nine times out of ten the consumer thinks it's his fault; or else, at the most, he sends you a few insults that don't reach you because of insufficient address. On the other hand, if an X-ray goes bad, after all that barium pap or the retrograde urography; and then a second goes bad, and the whole package of sheets; well, then that's not the end of it: trouble makes its own ascent, it grows as it climbs, and then drops on you like an affliction. All things which my predecessor had explained to me, with the typical didactic talent of the

Germans, in order to justify in my eyes the fantastic ritual of cleanliness which must be observed in the department, from beginning to end of the work process. I don't know if you're interested; just think that . . ."

I interrupted him: minute precautions, maniacal cleanliness, purity with eight zeroes, are things which make me suffer. I know very well that in some cases it is a matter of necessary measures, but I also know that, more often mania prevails over common sense, and alongside five sensible precepts or prohibitions lurk ten senseless, useless ones, which nobody dares rescind only out of mental laziness, superstition, or morbid fear of complications: even when it does not go so far as in military service, in which regulations serve to smuggle in a repressive discipline. Cerrato poured a drink for me: his big hand moved hesitantly to the neck of the bottle, as if the bottle was fluttering about the table to escape him; then he tilted it over my glass, banging against it several times. He agreed that things were often like that: for example, the women in the department of which he was telling me were forbidden to use face powder, but one time a compact had fallen out of a girl's pocket and opened, and quite a bit of powder had been wafted into the air; that day's production had been inspected with particular care, but it was perfect. Well, the prohibition against face powder still remained.

". . . but I have to tell you one detail, otherwise you won't understand the story. There is the religion of the hair (this is justified, I can assure you): the department is always slightly pressurized, and the air that is pumped in is carefully filtered. Over your clothes you wear a special overall and a cap over your hair: overalls and caps must be washed every day to remove lint or accidentally picked up hair. Shoes and stockings must be taken off at the entrance and are replaced by dustproof slippers.

"So there, that's the setting. I should add that for five or six years there had been no major accidents: an isolated complaint here and there from a few hospitals about altered sensitivity, but it was almost always a matter of products already past the expiration date. Troubles, I don't have to tell you, don't come at a gallop, like the Huns, but arrive quietly, stealthily, like epidemics. It began with a special-delivery letter from a diagnostic center in Vienna; it was couched in very civil terms. I would call it more a warning than a complaint, and attached as proof was an X ray: regular as regards grain and contrast but dotted with white, oblong spots the size of beans. We replied with a contrite letter in which we begged their pardon for the unintentional, etcetera, but after the first *Landsknecht** had died of the plague it is best not to entertain illusions: the plague is the plague, there's no point in playing the ostrich. The next week there were another two letters: one from Liège hinting at damages to be reimbursed, the other from the Soviet Union; I no longer remember (perhaps I have blocked it out) the complicated initials of the commercial agency that had sent it. When it was translated, everyone's hair stood on end. The fault, of course, was always the same, those dots shaped like beans, and the letter was very, very heavy: it spoke of three operations which had had to be postponed, of shifts lost, of tons of disputed sensitive paper, of an expert examination and an international controversy at the court of God knows where; and it enjoined us to send a *Spezialist* immediately.

"In such cases you try at least to lock the stable door after some of the cattle have escaped, but you don't always succeed. It being established that all the paper had passed the exit inspection, we therefore were dealing with a delayed defect that showed up while in the warehouse, ours or the customer's, or during transportation. The director called me in, discussed the case with me, very courteously, for two hours, but to me it seemed that he skinned me alive, slowly, methodically, and enjoyed doing it.

"We accepted the results of the laboratory inspection, and checked all the paper in stock batch by batch. The paper less

*Reference to the German soldiers who die of the plague in Manzoni's historical novel *The Betrothed*—TRANS.

than two months old was all right. In the rest the defect was found, though not in all: there were hundreds of batches, and about one-sixth showed the bean problem. My assistant, who was a young chemist and not very sharp, made a curious observation: the defective batches followed each other with a certain regularity, five good and one bad. It seemed to me a clue, and I tried to get to the bottom of it; that's how it was, exactly: almost all the spoiled paper was produced on Wednesday.

"I don't have to tell you that delayed troubles are by far the most pernicious. While you're searching for the causes, you still have to continue producing: but how can you be sure that the cause or causes are not still at work and the material you're producing is not the carrier of further disasters. Obviously you can keep it in quarantine for two months and inspect it again: But what are you going to tell the warehouses the world over that are not receiving the goods? And what about passive interests? And the name, the Good Name, the *Unbestrittener Ruf*, the unblemished reputation? And there's another complication: any change you might make in composition or technology must wait for two months before you know whether it helps or doesn't, whether it gets rid of the defect or accentuates it.

"I felt innocent, naturally: I had observed all the rules, I had not been lax in any way. Above me and below me, all the others felt just as innocent: those who had passed the raw materials as good, who had prepared and tested the emulsion of silver bromide, those who had wrapped, packed, and stored the packages of paper. I felt innocent, but I wasn't: I was guilty by definition, because the head of a department must answer for his department, and because where there's damage there's sin, and where there's sin there's a sinner. It's something exactly like original sin: you haven't done anything, but you're guilty and you must pay. Not with money, but worse: you lose sleep, lose your appetite, get an ulcer or shingles, and take a huge step toward terminal managerial neurosis.

"While complaining letters and telephone calls kept coming in, I persisted in trying to puzzle out that business of the

Wednesdays: it must surely have some significance. On Tuesday night a guard I didn't like had his shift—he had a scar on his chin and the face of a Nazi. I did not know whether or not to mention it to the director: to try to unload the blame on others is always bad policy. Then I had them bring me the payroll and saw that the Nazi had been with us only three months, while the bean trouble had begun to manifest itself on the paper produced ten months before. What new thing had occurred ten months before?

"About ten months before there had been accepted, after rigorous checks, a new supplier of the black paper which is used to protect the sensitive papers from light: but the defective material was proved to have been packed promiscuously in black paper coming from both suppliers. Also ten months before (nine, to be exact) a group of Turkish women workers had been hired; I interviewed them one by one, to their great amazement: I wanted to establish whether on Wednesday or Tuesday evening they did something different from usual. Did they wash, or did they *not* wash? Did they use some special cosmetic? Did they go dancing, and as a result sweat more than usual? I did not dare ask whether on Tuesday night they made love; in any event, I didn't get anywhere either directly or through the interpreter.

"Obviously, in the meanwhile the affair had become known throughout the factory, and people were looking at me in strange ways; also because I was the only Italian department head, and I could very well imagine the comments they must have exchanged behind my back. The decisive help came to me from one of the guards, who spoke a little Italian because he had fought in Italy: in fact he had been taken prisoner by the partisans around Biella and then exchanged for someone. He held no grudge, was loquacious, and spoke at random about a little of everything without ever coming to a conclusion: well, it was precisely his silly gabble that acted as Ariadne's thread. One day he told me that he was a fisherman, but that for almost a year now he no longer caught any fish in the small river nearby: ever since they had opened a tannery five or six kilometers upstream. He then told me that on certain days the water actually turned brown. There and then I didn't pay attention to his remarks, but I thought about them a few days later when from the window of my room in the guest house I saw the small truck bringing back the overalls from the laundry. I asked about it: the tannery had begun operating ten months before, and in fact the laundry washed the overalls in the water of the stream where the fisherman could no longer catch fish. However, they filtered it and made it pass through an ion exchange purifier. The overalls were washed during the day, they were dried at night in a dryer, and sent back early in the morning before the plant opened.

"I went to the tannery: I wanted to know when, where, how often, and on what days they emptied their vats. They sent me packing, but I returned two days later with the doctor from the Sanitation Office. Well, the largest of the tanning vats was emptied every week, on the night between Monday and Tuesday. They refused to tell me what it contained, but you know very well, organic tans are polyphenols and there is no ion exchange resin that can trap them, and what a polyphenol can do to silver bromide even you who are not in the field can imagine. I got a sample of the tanning solution, went to the experimental lab, and atomized a 1:10,000 solution in the darkroom in which was exposed a specimen of X-ray paper. The effect could be seen a few days later: the paper's sensitivity had disappeared, literally. The head of the lab did not believe his eyes. He told me that he had never seen so powerful an inhibitor. We tested it with increasingly diluted solutions, as homeopathic doctors do: with solutions of about one part to a million; we obtained bean-shaped spots, which, however, appeared only after two months of rest. The bean effect—*Bohneffekt*—had been reproduced in full: when all was said and done, it became obvious that a few thousand molecules of polyphenol absorbed by the fibers of the overalls during the wash and carried by an invisible piece of lint from the overall to the paper were enough to produce the spots."

The other dinner guests around us were talking noisily about children, vacations, salaries. We ended up by going off to the bar, where gradually we became sentimental and promised each other to renew a friendship that actually had never existed between us. We would keep in contact, and each of us would gather for the other more stories like this one, in which stolid matter manifests a cunning intent upon evil and obstruction, as if it revolted against the order dear to man: like those reckless outcasts, thirsting more for the ruination of others than for their own triumph, who in novels arrive from the ends of the earth to thwart the exploits of positive heroes.

VANADIUM

Varnish is an unstable substance by definition: in fact, at a
certain point in its career it must turn from a liquid into a solid.
But this must occur at the right time and place. If it doesn't, the
effects can be unpleasant or dramatic: it can happen that a
varnish hardens (we say brutally "monkeys") during its sojourn
in the warehouse, and in that case the merchandise must be
thrown out; or that the base resin hardens during the synthesis,
in a ten- or twenty-ton reactor, which amounts to a tragedy; or
even that the varnish does not harden at all, even after application, and then one becomes a laughingstock, since varnish that
doesn't dry is like a gun that doesn't shoot or a bull that can't
impregnate.

In many cases the oxygen in the air plays a part in the

hardening process. Among the various exploits, vital or destructive, which oxygen can perform, we varnish makers are interested above all in its capacity to react with certain small molecules such as those of certain oils, and of creating links between them, transforming them into a compact and therefore solid network. That is how, for example, linseed oil dries in the open air.

We had imported a shipment of resin for varnishes, indeed one of those resins which harden at an ordinary temperature by simple exposure to the atmosphere, and we were worried. Tested by itself, the resin dried as expected, but after having been ground up with a certain (irreplaceable) kind of lampblack, its ability to dry fell off to the point of disappearing: we had already set aside several tons of black paint which, despite all attempts to correct it, after application remained indefinitely sticky, like lugubrious flypaper.

In cases like these, before formulating accusations, one must proceed cautiously. The supplier was W., a large and respectable German company, one of the large segments into which, after the war, the Allies had dismembered the omnipotent IG-Farben: people like this, before admitting their guilt, throw on the scales all the weight of their prestige and all their ability at wearing you down. But there was no way to avoid the controversy: other shipments of resin behaved well with that same batch of lampblack, the resin was a special type that only W. produced, and we were bound by contract and absolutely had to continue supplying that black paint, without missing any due dates.

I wrote a well-mannered letter of protest, setting forth the terms of the problem, and a few days later the answer came: it was long and pedantic, advised obvious expedients and procedures which we had already adopted without result, and contained a superfluous and deliberately confused description of the mechanism of the resin's oxidation: it ignored our need for immediate action, and on the essential point simply stated that the relevant tests were under way. There was nothing left for us to do but immediately order another shipment, urging W. to check with particular care the resin's behavior with that kind of lampblack.

Together with the confirmation of this last order a second letter arrived, nearly as long as the first, and signed by the same Doktor L. Müller. It was a trifle more to the point than the first, recognized (with many qualifications and reservations) the justness of our grievance, and contained a piece of advice less obvious than the previous: "*ganz unerwarteterweise*," that is, in a completely unexpected fashion, the gnomes of their lab had discovered that the protested shipment was cured by the addition of 0.1 percent of vanadium naphthenate—an additive that until then had never been heard of in the world of varnishes. The unknown Dr. Müller urged us to check immediately on the truth of their statement; if the effect was confirmed, their observation could avoid for both parties the annoyances and hazards of an international dispute.

Müller. There was a Müller in my previous incarnation, but Müller is a very common name in Germany, like Molinari in Italy or Miller in English, of which it is an exact equivalent. Why continue to think about it? And yet, rereading the two letters with their heavy, lumbering phrasing encumbered with technical jargon, I could not quiet a doubt, the kind that refuses to be pushed aside and rasps slightly within you, like termites. Oh, come now, there must be two hundred thousand Müllers in Germany, forget it and think about the varnish that has to be corrected.

. . . and then, all of a sudden, there rose before my eyes a detail of the last letter which had escaped me: it was not a typing mistake, it was repeated twice; it said "naptenate," not "naphthenate" as it should be. Now I conserve pathologically precise memories of my encounters in that by now remote world: well, that other Müller too, in an unforgotten lab full of freezing cold, hope, and fear, used to say "beta-Naptylamin" instead of "beta-Naphthylamin."

The Russians were knocking at the door, two or three times a day Allied planes came to shake apart the Buna plant: there was no water, steam, or electricity; not a single pane of glass was intact; but the order was to begin producing Buna rubber, and Germans do not discuss orders.

I was in a laboratory with two other skilled prisoners, similar to those educated slaves that the rich Romans imported from Greece. To work was as impossible as it was futile: our time was almost entirely spent dismantling the apparatus at every air-raid alarm and putting them together again at the all-clear. But as I said, orders are not discussed, and every so often some inspector burrowed through the rubble and snow all the way to us to make sure that the lab's work proceeded according to instructions. Sometimes an SS with a stone face would come, at other times a little old soldier from the local militia who was timid as a mouse, and at other times still a civilian. The civilian who appeared most often was called Dr. Müller.

He must have been a person of some authority because everybody saluted him first. He was a tall, corpulent man of about forty, more coarse than refined in appearance. He had spoken to me only three times, and all three times with a timidity rare in that place, as if he were ashamed of something. The first time only about the work (the dosage of the "Naptylamin," in fact); the second time he had asked me why I had so long a beard, to which I had replied that none of us had a razor, in fact not even a handkerchief, and that our beards were shaved officially every Monday; the third time he had given me a note, written neatly on a typewriter, which authorized me to shave also on Thursday and to be issued by the *Effektenmagazin* a pair of leather shoes and had asked me, addressing me formally, "Why do you look so perturbed?" I, who at that time thought in German, had said to myself, *"Der Mann hat keine Ahnung"* (This fellow hasn't got an inkling).

Duty first. I hastened to track down among our usual suppliers a sample of vanadium naphthenate, and found out that it wasn't easy: the product was not in regular production, was prepared only in small quantities and only on order; I put through an order.

The return of that "pt" had thrown me into a state of violent agitation. To find myself, man to man, having a reckoning with one of the "others" had been my keenest and most constant desire since I had left the concentration camp. It had been met only in part by letters from my German readers: they did not satisfy me, those honest, generalized declarations of repentance and solidarity on the part of people I had never seen, whose other face I did not know, and who probably were not implicated except emotionally. The encounter I looked forward to with so much intensity as to dream of it (in German) at night, was an encounter with one of them down there, who had disposed of us, who had not looked into our eyes, as though we didn't have eyes. Not to take my revenge: I am not the Count of Montecristo. Only to reestablish the right proportions, and to say, "Well?" If this Müller was my Müller, he was not the perfect antagonist, because in some way, perhaps only for a moment, he had felt pity, or just only a rudiment of professional solidarity. Perhaps even less: perhaps he had only resented the fact that the strange hybrid of colleague and instrument that after all was a chemist frequented a laboratory without the *Anstand*, the decorum, that the laboratory demands; but the others around him had not even felt this. He was not the perfect antagonist: but, as is known, perfection belongs to narrated events, not to those we live.

I got in touch with W.'s representatives, whom I knew quite well, and asked him to look with discretion into Dr. Müller: How old was he? What did he look like? Where had he been during the war? The answer was not long in coming: his age and appearance coincided, the man had worked first at Schkopau to get experience in rubber technology, then at the Buna factory near Auschwitz. I obtained his address and sent him, from one private person to another, a copy of the German edition of *If This Is a Man*, with an accompanying letter in which I asked him   *215* if he was really the Müller of Auschwitz, and if he remembered "the three men of the laboratory"; well, I hoped he would pardon this crude intrusion and return from the void but I was one of the three, besides being the customer worried about the resin that did not dry.

I began to wait for the reply, while on the company level there continued, like the oscillation of an enormous, very slow pendulum, the exchange of chemico-bureaucratic letters concerning the Italian vanadium that did not work as well as the German. Would you please in the meantime be so kind as to send us urgently the specifications of the product and ship to us by air freight 50 kilograms, whose cost you will deduct, etc.? On the technical level the matter seemed set on the right course, but the fate of the defective shipment was not clear: to hold on to it at a discount, or return it at W.'s expense, or ask for arbitration. Meanwhile, as is the custom, we threatened each other with legal action, *"gerichtlich vorzugehen."*

The "private" reply still kept me waiting, which was almost as irritating and nerve-racking as the company dispute. What did I know about my man? Nothing—in all probability he had blotted everything out, deliberately or not; for him my letter and my book were an ill-mannered and irksome intrusion, a clumsy invitation to stir up a by now well settled sediment, an assault on *Anstand*. He would never reply. A pity: he was not a perfect German, but do perfect Germans exist? Or perfect Jews? They are an abstraction: the transition from the general to the particular always has stimulating surprises in store, when the interlocutor without contours, ghostly, takes shape before you, gradually or at a single blow, and becomes the *Mitmensch*, the co-man, with all his depth, his tics, anomalies, and incoherences. By now almost two months had passed: the reply would no longer arrive. Too bad.

It arrived dated March 2, 1967, on elegant paper headed with vaguely Gothic characters. It was a preliminary letter, brief and reserved. Yes, the Müller of Buna was indeed he. He had read my book, recognized with emotion persons and places; he was happy to know that I had survived; he asked for information about the other two "men of the laboratory," and up to this point there was nothing strange, since they were named in the book: but he also asked about Goldbaum, whom I had not named. He added that he had reread, for the occasion, his notes on that period: he would gladly discuss them with me in a hoped-for personal meeting, "useful both to myself and to you, and necessary for the purpose of overcoming that terrible past" (*"im Sinne der Bewältigung der so furchtbaren Vergangenheit"*). He declared at the end that, among all the prisoners he had met at Auschwitz, I was the one who had made the strongest and most lasting impression, but this could well be flattery: from the tone of the letter, and especially from that sentence about "overcoming," it seemed that the man expected something from me.

Now it was up to me to reply, and I felt embarrassed. You see, the undertaking had succeeded, the adversary was snared; he was there before me, almost a colleague varnish maker, he wrote like me on paper with a letterhead, and he even remembered Goldbaum. He was still quite blurred, but it was obvious that he wanted from me something like an absolution, because he had a past to overcome and I didn't: I wanted from him only a discount on the bill for the defective resin. The situation was interesting but atypical: it coincided only in part with that of the reprobate hauled before a judge.

First of all: In what language should I reply? Certainly not in German; I would have made ridiculous mistakes, which my role did not permit. Better always to fight on your terrain: I wrote to him in Italian. The two men of the laboratory were dead, I did not know where or how; the same for Goldbaum, who died of cold and hunger during the evacuation march. As for me, he knew the essentials from my book, and from my business correspondence about the vanadium.

I had many questions to ask him: too many, and too heavy for him and for me. Why Auschwitz? Why Pannwitz? Why the children in the gas chambers? But I felt that it was not yet the moment to go beyond certain limits, and I asked him only *217* whether he accepted the judgments, implicit and explicit, of my book. Whether he felt that IG-Farben had spontaneously taken on the slave labor force. Whether he knew then about Auschwitz's "installations," which devoured ten thousand lives a day only seven kilometers away from the Buna rubber plant. And finally, since he had talked about his "notations of that period," would he send me a copy?

About the "hoped-for meeting" I said nothing, because I was afraid of it. No point in having recourse to euphemisms, to talk about shyness, disgust, reticence. Fear was the word: just as I didn't feel myself to be a Montecristo, so I didn't feel myself to be Horatius-Curiatius. I did not feel capable of representing the dead of Auschwitz, nor did it seem to me sensible to see in Müller the representative of the butchers. I know myself: I do not possess any polemical skill, my opponent distracts me, he interests me more as a man than as an opponent, I take pains to listen and run the risk of believing him; indignation and the correct judgment return later, on the way downstairs, when they are no longer of any use. It was best for me to stick to writing.

Müller wrote to me on the company level that the fifty kilos had been shipped, and that W. was sure of a friendly settlement, etcetera. Almost simultaneously there arrived at my house the letter I expected; but it was not what I expected. It was not a model letter, paradigmatic: at this point, if this story were invented, I would have been able to introduce only two kinds of letters: a humble, warm, Christian letter, from a redeemed German; a ribald, proud, glacial letter from an obdurate Nazi. Now this story is not invented, and reality is always more complex than invention: less kempt, cruder, less rounded out. It rarely lies on one level.

The letter was eight pages long and contained a photograph that shook me. The face was *that* face: grown old and at the same time ennobled by a skillful photographer; I could hear him again high above me pronounce those words of distracted and momentary compassion: "Why do you look so perturbed?"

It was visibly the work of an inept writer: rhetorical, sincere only by half, full of digressions and farfetched praise, moving, pedantic, and clumsy: it defied any summary, all-encompassing judgment.

He attributed the events at Auschwitz to Man, without differentiation; he deplored them and found consolation in the thought of the other men spoken of in my book, Alberto, Lorenzo, "against whom the weapons of the night are blunted": the phrase was mine, but repeated by him it struck me as hypocritical and jarring. He told his story: "dragged initially along by the general enthusiasm for Hitler's regime," he had joined a nationalistic student league, which soon after was by mandate incorporated in the SA; he had managed to be discharged and observed that "this too was therefore possible." When the war came he had been mobilized in the antiaircraft corps, and only then, confronted by the ruins of the city, had he experienced "shame and indignation" about the war. In May of 1944 he had been able (like me!) to have his status as a chemist recognized, and he had been assigned to the Schkopau factory of IG-Farben, of which the plant at Auschwitz was an enlarged copy: at Schkopau he had trained a group of Ukrainian girls for work in the lab, girls whom in fact I had met again in Auschwitz and whose strange familiarity with Dr. Müller I could not then explain. He had been transferred to Auschwitz together with the girls only in November 1944: at that time the name of Auschwitz did not have any significance, either for him or his acquaintances; on his arrival, he had had a brief introductory meeting with the technical director (presumably Engineer Faust), who warned him that "the Jews in Buna must be assigned only the most menial tasks, and compassion was not tolerated."

He had been assigned to work directly under Dr. Pannwitz, the man who had put me through a peculiar "state exam" to ascertain my professional abilities. Müller made it clear that he had a very low opinion of his superior, and informed me that the man had died of a brain tumor in 1946. It was he, Müller, who had been in charge of the organization of the Buna lab; he stated that he had known nothing about that exam, and that he himself had chosen us three specialists, and me in particular; according to this information, improbable but not impossible, I was therefore in debt to him for my survival. He affirmed that he had had a relationship with me almost of friendship between equals; that he had conversed with me about scientific problems and had meditated, on this occasion, on what "precious human values are destroyed by other men out of pure brutality." Not only did I not remember any such conversations (and my memory of that period, as I have said, is excellent), but against the background of disintegration, mutual distrust, and mortal weariness, the mere supposition of them was totally outside reality, and could only be explained by a very naive ex post facto wishful thinking; perhaps it was an incident he told a lot of people and did not realize I was the one person in the world who could not believe it. Perhaps in good faith he had constructed a convenient past for himself. He did not remember the two details about the shaving and the shoes, but he remembered others, similar and, in my opinion, quite plausible. He had heard about my scarlet fever and had worried about my survival, especially when he learned that the prisoners were being evacuated on foot. On January 26, 1945, he had been assigned by the SS to the Volkssturm, the tatterdemalion army of rejects, old men, and children who were supposed to block the Soviet advance. Luckily, he had been saved by the aforementioned technical director, who had authorized him to run off to a rear area.

To my question about IG-Farben he answered curtly that, yes, it had employed prisoners, but only to protect them: actually, he put forward the (insane!) opinion that the entire Buna-Monowitz plant, eight square kilometers of giant buildings, had been constructed with the intention of "protecting the Jews and contributing to their survival," and that the order not to have compassion for them was *"eine Tarnung"* ("camouflage"). *Nihil de principe*, no accusation against IG-Farben: my man was still an employee of W., which was its heir, and you do not spit into your own dish. During his brief sojourn at Auschwitz he "had never gained knowledge of any proviso that seemed aimed at the killing of Jews." Paradoxical, offensive, but not to be excluded: at that time, among the German silent majority, the common technique was to try to know as little as possible, and therefore not to ask questions. He too, obviously, had not demanded explanations from anyone, not even from himself, although on clear days the flames of the crematorium were visible from the Buna factory.

A little before the final collapse he had been captured by the Americans and locked up for a few days in a camp for prisoners of war that he, with unwitting irony, described as being "primitively equipped"; just as at the time of our meeting in the lab, so now as he wrote, Müller apparently continued not to have an inkling—*"keine Ahnung."* He had returned to his family at the end of June 1945. And this, substantially, was the content of his notations, which I had asked to see.

He perceived in my book an overcoming of Judaism, a fulfillment of the Christian precept to love one's enemies, and a testimony of faith in Man, and he concluded by insisting on the necessity of a meeting, in Germany or Italy, where he was ready to join me when and where I wished: preferably on the Riviera. Two days later, through company channels, a letter arrived from W. which, surely not by chance, bore the same date as the long private letter, and also the same signature; it was a conciliatory letter, they recognized that the fault was theirs, and declared themselves open to any proposal. They implied that all is well that ends well; the incident had brought to light the virtues of vanadium naphthenate, which from now on would be incorporated directly into the resin for all customers.

What to do? The Müller character was *"entpuppt,"* he had come out of his chrysalis, he was sharply defined, in perfect focus. Neither infamous nor a hero: after filtering off the rhetoric and the lies in good or bad faith there remained a typically gray human specimen, one of the not so few one-eyed *221* men in the kingdom of the blind. He did me an undeserved honor in attributing to me the virtue of loving my enemies: no, despite the distant privileges he had reserved for me, and although he had not been an enemy in the strict sense of the word, I did not feel like loving him. I did not love him, and I didn't want to see him, and yet I felt a certain measure of respect for him: it is not easy to be one-eyed. He was not cowardly, or deaf, or a cynic, he had not conformed, he was trying to settle his accounts with the past and they didn't tally: he tried to make them tally, perhaps by cheating a little bit. Could one ask much more from an ex-SA? The comparison, which so many times I had the opportunity to make, with other honest Germans met on the beach or in the factory, was all in his favor: his condemnation of Nazism was timid and evasive, but he had not sought justifications. He sought a colloquy: he had a conscience, and he struggled to soothe it. In his first letter he had spoken of "overcoming the past," *"Bewältigung der Vergangenheit"*: I later found out that this is a stereotyped phrase, a euphemism in today's Germany, where it is universally understood as "redemption from Nazism"; but the root *walt* that it contains also appears in the words that express "domination," "violence," and "rape," and I believe that translating the expression with "distortion of the past" or "violence done to the past" would not stray very far from its profound meaning. And yet this taking shelter in commonplaces was better than the florid obtuseness of the other Germans: his efforts to overcome were clumsy, a bit ridiculous, irritating and sad, and yet decorous. And didn't he get me a pair of shoes?

On my first free Sunday I set about, full of perplexity, preparing a reply as sincere as possible, balanced and dignified. I made a draft: I thanked him for having taken me into the lab; I declared myself ready to forgive my enemies, and perhaps even to love them, but only when they showed certain signs of repentance, that is, when they ceased being enemies. In the opposite case, that of the enemy who remains an enemy, who perseveres in his desire to inflict suffering, it is certain that one must not forgive him: one can try to salvage him, one can (one must!) discuss with him, but it is our duty to judge him, not to forgive him. As to the specific judgment on his behavior, which Müller implicitly asked of me, I tactfully cited two cases known to me of his German colleagues who in their actions toward us had done something much more courageous than what he claimed to have done. I admitted that we are not all born heroes, and that a world in which everyone would be like him, that is, honest and unarmed, would be tolerable, but this is an unreal world. In the real world the armed exist, they build Auschwitz, and the honest and unarmed clear the road for them; therefore every German must answer for Auschwitz, indeed every man, and after Auschwitz it is no longer permissible to be unarmed. I did not say a word about the meeting on the Riviera.

That same evening Müller called me on the telephone from Germany. The connection was bad, and in any event by now it is no longer easy for me to understand German on the telephone: his voice was labored and seemed broken, his tone tense and agitated. He announced that for Pentecost, within six weeks, he would come to Finale Ligure: Could we meet? Taken unawares, I said yes. I asked him to let me know beforehand the details of his arrival and put aside my now superfluous draft.

Eight days later I received from Mrs. Müller the announcement of the unexpected death of Doktor Lothar Müller in his sixtieth year of life.

CARBON

The reader, at this point, will have realized for some time now that this is not a chemical treatise: my presumption does not reach so far—*"ma voix est foible, et même un peu profane."* Nor is it an autobiography, save in the partial and symbolic limits in which every piece of writing is autobiographical, indeed every human work; but it is in some fashion a history.

It is—or would have liked to be—a micro-history, the history of a trade and its defeats, victories, and miseries, such as everyone wants to tell when he feels close to concluding the arc of his career, and art ceases to be long. Having reached this point in life, what chemist, facing the Periodic Table, or the monumental indices of Beilstein or Landolt, does not perceive scattered among them the sad tatters, or trophies, of his own professional past? He only has to leaf through any treatise and memories rise up in bunches: there is among us he who has tied his destiny, indelibly, to bromine or to propylene, or the -NCO group, or glutamic acid; and every chemistry student, faced by almost any treatise, should be aware that on one of those pages, perhaps in a single line, formula, or word, his future is written in indecipherable characters, which, however, will become clear "afterward": after success, error, or guilt, victory or defeat. Every no longer young chemist, turning again to the *verhängnisvoll* page in that same treatise, is struck by love or disgust, delights or despairs.

So it happens, therefore, that every element says something to someone (something different to each) like the mountain valleys or beaches visited in youth. One must perhaps make an exception for carbon, because it says everything to everyone, that is, it is not specific, in the same way that Adam is not specific as an ancestor—unless one discovers today (why not?) the chemist-stylite who has dedicated his life to graphite or the diamond. And yet it is exactly to this carbon that I have an old debt, contracted during what for me were decisive days. To carbon, the element of life, my first literary dream was turned, insistently dreamed in an hour and a place when my life was not worth much: yes, I wanted to tell the story of an atom of carbon.

Is it right to speak of a "particular" atom of carbon? For the chemist there exist some doubts, because until 1970 he did not have the techniques permitting him to see, or in any event isolate, a single atom; no doubts exist for the narrator, who therefore sets out to narrate.

Our character lies for hundreds of millions of years, bound to three atoms of oxygen and one of calcium, in the form of limestone: it already has a very long cosmic history behind it, but we shall ignore it. For it time does not exist, or exists only in the form of sluggish variations in temperature, daily or seasonal, if, for the good fortune of this tale, its position is not too far from the earth's surface. Its existence, whose monotony cannot be thought of without horror, is a pitiless alternation of hots and colds, that is, of oscillations (always of equal frequency) a trifle more restricted and a trifle more ample: an imprisonment, for this potentially living personage, worthy of the Catholic Hell. To it, until this moment, the present tense is suited, which is that of description, rather than the past tense, which is that of narration—it is congealed in an eternal present, barely scratched by the moderate quivers of thermal agitation.

But, precisely for the good fortune of the narrator, whose story could otherwise have come to an end, the limestone rock ledge of which the atom forms a part lies on the surface. It lies within reach of man and his pickax (all honor to the pickax and its modern equivalents; they are still the most important intermediaries in the millenial dialogue between the elements and man): at any moment—which I, the narrator, decide out of pure caprice to be the year 1840—a blow of the pickax detached it and sent it on its way to the lime kiln, plunging it into the world of things that change. It was roasted until it separated from the calcium, which remained so to speak with its feet on the ground and went to meet a less brilliant destiny, which we shall not narrate. Still firmly clinging to two of its three former oxygen companions, it issued from the chimney and took the path of the air. Its story, which once was immobile, now turned tumultuous.

It was caught by the wind, flung down on the earth, lifted ten kilometers high. It was breathed in by a falcon, descending into its precipitous lungs, but did not penetrate its rich blood and was expelled. It dissolved three times in the water of the sea, once in the water of a cascading torrent, and again was expelled. It traveled with the wind for eight years: now high, now low, on the sea and among the clouds, over forests, deserts, and limitless expanses of ice; then it stumbled into capture and the organic adventure.

Carbon, in fact, is a singular element: it is the only element

that can bind itself in long stable chains without a great expense of energy, and for life on earth (the only one we know so far) precisely long chains are required. Therefore carbon is the key element of living substance: but its promotion, its entry into the living world, is not easy and must follow an obligatory, intricate path, which has been clarified (and not yet definitively) only in recent years. If the elaboration of carbon were not a common daily occurrence, on the scale of billions of tons a week, wherever the green of a leaf appears, it would by full right deserve to be called a miracle.

The atom we are speaking of, accompanied by its two satellites which maintained it in a gaseous state, was therefore borne by the wind along a row of vines in the year 1848. It had the good fortune to brush against a leaf, penetrate it, and be nailed there by a ray of the sun. If my language here becomes imprecise and allusive, it is not only because of my ignorance: this decisive event, this instantaneous work *a tre*—of the carbon dioxide, the light, and the vegetal greenery—has not yet been described in definitive terms, and perhaps it will not be for a long time to come, so different is it from that other "organic" chemistry which is the cumbersome, slow, and ponderous work of man: and yet this refined, minute, and quick-witted chemistry was "invented" two or three billion years ago by our silent sisters, the plants, which do not experiment and do not discuss, and whose temperature is identical to that of the environment in which they live. If to comprehend is the same as forming an image, we will never form an image of a happening* whose scale is a millionth of a millimeter, whose rhythm is a millionth of a second, and whose protagonists are in their essence invisible. Every verbal description must be inadequate, and one will be as good as the next, so let us settle for the following description.

Our atom of carbon enters the leaf, colliding with other innumerable (but here useless) molecules of nitrogen and oxygen. It adheres to a large and complicated molecule that activates it, and simultaneously receives the decisive message from the sky,

*English in original—TRANS.

in the flashing form of a packet of solar light: in an instant, like an insect caught by a spider, it is separated from its oxygen, combined with hydrogen and (one thinks) phosphorus, and finally inserted in a chain, whether long or short does not matter, but it is the chain of life. All this happens swiftly, in silence, at the temperature and pressure of the atmosphere, and gratis: dear colleagues, when we learn to do likewise we will be *sicut Deus*, and we will have also solved the problem of hunger in the world.

But there is more and worse, to our shame and that of our art. Carbon dioxide, that is, the aerial form of the carbon of which we have up till now spoken: this gas which constitutes the raw material of life, the permanent store upon which all that grows draws, and the ultimate destiny of all flesh, is not one of the principal components of air but rather a ridiculous remnant, an "impurity," thirty times less abundant than argon, which nobody even notices. The air contains 0.03 percent; if Italy was air, the only Italians fit to build life would be, for example, the fifteen thousand inhabitants of Milazzo in the province of Messina. This, on the human scale, is ironic acrobatics, a juggler's trick, an incomprehensible display of omnipotence-arrogance, since from this ever renewed impurity of the air we come, we animals and we plants, and we the human species, with our four billion discordant opinions, our milleniums of history, our wars and shames, nobility and pride. In any event, our very presence on the planet becomes laughable in geometric terms: if all of humanity, about 250 million tons, were distributed in a layer of homogeneous thickness on all the emergent lands, the "stature of man" would not be visible to the naked eye; the thickness one would obtain would be around sixteen thousandths of a millimeter.

Now our atom is inserted: it is part of a structure, in an architectural sense; it has become related and tied to five companions so identical with it that only the fiction of the story permits me to distinguish them. It is a beautiful ring-shaped structure, an almost regular hexagon, which however is subjected to complicated exchanges and balances with the water in which it is dissolved; because by now it is dissolved in water, indeed in the sap of the vine, and this, to remain dissolved, is both the obligation and the privilege of all substances that are destined (I was about to say "wish") to change. And if then anyone really wanted to find out why a ring, and why a hexagon, and why soluble in water, well, he need not worry: these are among the not many questions to which our doctrine can reply with a persuasive discourse, accessible to everyone, but out of place here.

It has entered to form part of a molecule of glucose, just to speak plainly: a fate that is neither fish, flesh, nor fowl, which is intermediary, which prepares it for its first contact with the animal world but does not authorize it to take on a higher responsibility: that of becoming part of a proteic edifice. Hence it travels, at the slow pace of vegetal juices, from the leaf through the pedicel and by the shoot to the trunk, and from here descends to the almost ripe bunch of grapes. What then follows is the province of the winemakers: we are only interested in pinpointing the fact that it escaped (to our advantage, since we would not know how to put it in words) the alcoholic fermentation, and reached the wine without changing its nature.

It is the destiny of wine to be drunk, and it is the destiny of glucose to be oxidized. But it was not oxidized immediately: its drinker kept it in his liver for more than a week, well curled up and tranquil, as a reserve aliment for a sudden effort; an effort that he was forced to make the following Sunday, pursuing a bolting horse. Farewell to the hexagonal structure: in the space of a few instants the skein was unwound and became glucose again, and this was dragged by the bloodstream all the way to a minute muscle fiber in the thigh, and here brutally split into two molecules of lactic acid, the grim harbinger of fatigue: only later, some minutes after, the panting of the lungs was able to supply the oxygen necessary to quietly oxidize the latter. So a new molecule of carbon dioxide returned to the atmosphere, and a parcel of the energy that the sun had handed to the vine-shoot passed from the state of chemical energy to that of mechanical energy, and thereafter settled down in the slothful condition of heat, warming up imperceptibly the air moved by the running and the blood of the runner. "Such is life," although rarely is it described in this manner: an inserting itself, a drawing off to its advantage, a parasitizing of the downward course of energy, from its noble solar form to the degraded one of low-temperature heat. In this downward course, which leads to equilibrium and thus death, life draws a bend and nests in it.

Our atom is again carbon dioxide, for which we apologize: this too is an obligatory passage; one can imagine and invent others, but on earth that's the way it is. Once again the wind, which this time travels far; sails over the Apennines and the Adriatic, Greece, the Aegean, and Cyprus: we are over Lebanon, and the dance is repeated. The atom we are concerned with is now trapped in a structure that promises to last for a long time: it is the venerable trunk of a cedar, one of the last; it is passed again through the stages we have already described, and the glucose of which it is a part belongs, like the bead of a rosary, to a long chain of cellulose. This is no longer the hallucinatory and geological fixity of rock, this is no longer millions of years, but we can easily speak of centuries because the cedar is a tree of great longevity. It is our whim to abandon it for a year or five hundred years: let us say that after twenty years (we are in 1868) a wood worm has taken an interest in it. It has dug its tunnel between the trunk and the bark, with the obstinate and blind voracity of its race; as it drills it grows, and its tunnel grows with it. There it has swallowed and provided a setting for the subject of this story; then it has formed a pupa, and in the spring it has come out in the shape of an ugly gray moth which is now drying in the sun, confused and dazzled by the splendor of the day. Our atom is in one of the insect's thousand eyes, contributing to the summary and crude vision with which it orients itself in space. The insect is fecundated, lays its eggs, and dies: the small cadaver lies in the undergrowth of the woods, it is emptied of its fluids, but the chitin carapace resists for a long time, almost indestructible. The snow and sun return above it without injuring it: it is buried by the dead leaves and the loam, it has become a slough, a "thing," but the death of atoms, unlike ours, is never irrevocable. Here are at work the omnipresent, untiring, and invisible gravediggers of the undergrowth, the microorganisms of the humus. The carapace, with its eyes by now blind, has slowly disintegrated, and the ex-drinker, ex-cedar, ex-wood worm has once again taken wing.

We will let it fly three times around the world, until 1960, and in justification of so long an interval in respect to the human measure we will point out that it is, however, much shorter than the average: which, we understand, is two hundred years. Every two hundred years, every atom of carbon that is not congealed in materials by now stable (such as, precisely, limestone, or coal, or diamond, or certain plastics) enters and reenters the cycle of life, through the narrow door of photosynthesis. Do other doors exist? Yes, some syntheses created by man; they are a title of nobility for man-the-maker, but until now their quantitative importance is negligible. They are doors still much narrower than that of the vegetal greenery; knowingly or not, man has not tried until now to compete with nature on this terrain, that is, he has not striven to draw from the carbon dioxide in the air the carbon that is necessary to nourish him, clothe him, warm him, and for the hundred other more sophisticated needs of modern life. He has not done it because he has not needed to: he has found, and is still finding (but for how many more decades?) gigantic reserves of carbon already organicized, or at least reduced. Besides the vegetable and animal worlds, these reserves are constituted by deposits of coal and petroleum: but these too are the inheritance of photosynthetic activity carried out in distant epochs, so that one can well affirm that photosynthesis is not only the sole path by which carbon becomes living matter, but also the sole path by which the sun's energy becomes chemically usable.

231

It is possible to demonstrate that this completely arbitrary story is nevertheless true. I could tell innumerable other stories, and they would all be true: all literally true, in the nature of the transitions, in their order and data. The number of atoms is so great that one could always be found whose story coincides with any capriciously invented story. I could recount an endless number of stories about carbon atoms that become colors or perfumes in flowers; of others which, from tiny algae to small crustaceans to fish, gradually return as carbon dioxide to the waters of the sea, in a perpetual, frightening round-dance of life and death, in which every devourer is immediately devoured; of others which instead attain a decorous semi-eternity in the yellowed pages of some archival document, or the canvas of a famous painter; or those to which fell the privilege of forming part of a grain of pollen and left their fossil imprint in the rocks for our curiosity; of others still that descended to become part of the mysterious shape-messengers of the human seed, and participated in the subtle process of division, duplication, and fusion from which each of us is born. Instead, I will tell just one more story, the most secret, and I will tell it with the humility and restraint of him who knows from the start that his theme is desperate, his means feeble, and the trade of clothing facts in words is bound by its very nature to fail.

It is again among us, in a glass of milk. It is inserted in a very complex, long chain, yet such that almost all of its links are acceptable to the human body. It is swallowed; and since every living structure harbors a savage distrust toward every contribution of any material of living origin, the chain is meticulously broken apart and the fragments, one by one, are accepted or rejected. One, the one that concerns us, crosses the intestinal threshold and enters the bloodstream: it migrates, knocks at the door of a nerve cell, enters, and supplants the carbon which was part of it. This cell belongs to a brain, and it is my brain, the brain of the *me* who is writing; and the cell in question, and within it the atom in question, is in charge of my writing, in a gigantic minuscule game which nobody has yet described. It is that which at this instant, issuing out of a labyrinthine tangle of yeses and nos, makes my hand run along a certain path on the paper, mark it with these volutes that are signs: a double snap, up and down, between two levels of energy, guides this hand of mine to impress on the paper this dot, here, this one.